MACMILLAN

LANGUAGE ARTS TODAY

Good stories are fun to read. When the artist Don Daily read *Blue Rocket Fun Show* by Thomas P. Lewis, he decided to draw a picture. He drew the picture on the cover of your book. The story begins on page 302. We hope that you like the story, too!

SENIOR AUTHORS

ANN McCALLUM   WILLIAM STRONG   TINA THOBURN   PEGGY WILLIAMS

Literature Consultant for Macmillan Language Arts and Macmillan Reading   Joan Glazer

Macmillan Publishing Company   **New York**
Collier Macmillan Publishers   **London**

ACKNOWLEDGMENTS

The publisher gratefully acknowledges permission to reprint the following copyrighted material:

"The Blue Rocket Fun Show" is excerpted from *The Blue Rocket Fun Show or, Friends Forever* by Thomas P. Lewis. Text copyright © 1986 by Thomas P. Lewis. Reprinted and recorded by permission of Macmillan Publishing Company.

"Cherries and Cherry Pits" from *Cherries and Cherry Pits* by Vera B. Williams. Copyright © 1986 by Vera B. Williams. By permission of Greenwillow Books (A Division of William Morrow and Company, Inc.)

"Happy Birthday, Mole and Troll" is the chapter "Happy Birthday" in *Happy Birthday, Mole and Troll* by Tony Johnston, illustrated by Cindy Szekeres. Text copyright © 1979 by Tony Johnston. Illustrations copyright © 1979 by Cindy Szekeres. Reprinted and recorded by permission of G.P. Putnam's Sons. Reprinted also by permission of Curtis Brown Ltd.

"Max" from *Max* by Rachel Isadora. Copyright © 1976 by Rachel Isadora. Reprinted by permission of Macmillan Publishing Company. Recorded by permission of the publisher.

"We Are Best Friends" from *We Are Best Friends* by Aliki. Copyright © 1982 by Aliki Brandenberg. By permission of Greenwillow Books (A Division of William Morrow & Company, Inc.). By permission also of the Bodley Head, London.

Poems and Brief Quotations

"The Animal Store" from *Taxis and Toadstools* by Rachel Field. Copyright © 1926 by Doubleday, a division of Bantam, Doubleday, Dell Publishing Group, Inc. Reprinted by permission of the publisher. By permission also of World Book Ltd., London. Recorded by permission of Doubleday.

Excerpt from *Georgia Music* by Helen V. Griffith. Copyright © 1986 by Helen V. Griffith. Reprinted and recorded by permission of Greenwillow Books (A Division of William Morrow and Company, Inc.).

Excerpt from *Happy Birthday, Grampie* by Susan Pearson. Text copyright © 1987 by Susan Pearson. Reprinted and recorded by permission of the publisher, Dial Books for Young Readers.

Specified excerpt from *Happy Birthday to You!* by Dr. Seuss. Copyright © 1959 by Dr. Seuss. Reprinted by permission of Random House, Inc. and International Creative Management.

Riddles 1, 3, and 15 from *Unriddling* by Alvin Schwartz (J. B. Lippincott). Text copyright © 1983 by Alvin Schwartz. Reprinted by permission of Harper & Row, Publishers, Inc. and Curtis Brown, Ltd.

Excerpt from *Zero Is Not Nothing* by Mindel and Harry Sitomer (Thomas Y. Crowell). Text copyright © 1978 by Mindel and Harry Sitomer. Reprinted by permission of Harper & Row, Publishers, Inc.

"Sleeping Outdoors" from *Rhymes About Us* by Marchette Chute. Copyright © 1974 by E. P. Dutton, Inc. Reprinted by permission of the author.

Excerpt from *Science Fun with Mud and Dirt* by Rose Wyler. Copyright © 1986 by Rose Wyler. Reprinted by permission of Simon & Schuster, Inc.

"Song for a Hot Day" from *Summer Green* by Elizabeth Coatsworth.

Copyright © 1948 by Macmillan Publishing Company, renewed 1975 by Elizabeth Coatsworth Beston. Reprinted with the permission of Macmillan Publishing Company. Recorded by permission of Mrs. Kay Barnes and Mrs. Margaret B. Mechau.

"The Song of the Sour Plum" from *The Song of the Sour Plum* translated by Ann Herring. English translation copyright © 1968 by Ann Herring. Reprinted and recorded by permission of Fukuinkan Shoten.

Excerpt from "This Book Belongs to Me!" by Arnold Lobel in *Once Upon a Time*. Copyright © 1986 by G. P. Putnam's Sons. Reprinted by permission.

Excerpt from "Valentine for Earth" (and entire poem) from *The Little Naturalist* by Frances Frost. Copyright © 1959 by the Estate of Frances Frost & Kurt Werth. Originally published by McGraw-Hill Book Company.

"Whistle Wish" by Constance Andrea Keremes. Reprinted by permission of the author.

"A Wish Is Quite a Tiny Thing" from *Days and Days* by Annette Wynne (J. B. Lippincott). Copyright 1919 by Harper & Row, Publishers, Inc. Renewed 1947 by Annette Wynne. Reprinted by permission of Harper & Row, Publishers, Inc.

"Wishing" from *Jamboree: Rhymes for All Times* by Eve Merriam. Copyright © 1962, 1964, 1966, 1973, 1984 by Eve Merriam. All rights reserved. Reprinted by permission of Marian Reiner for the author.

"Merry-Go-Round" from *I Like Machinery* by Dorothy W. Baruch. Permission granted by Bertha Klausner International Literary Agency.

Excerpt from *My Prairie Year* by Brett Harvey. Copyright © 1986 by Brett Harvey. All rights reserved. Reprinted by permission of Holiday House, Inc.

Excerpt from (and entire) poem #12 ("Come out and ride....") from *Any Me I Want to Be* by Karla Kuskin. Copyright © 1972 by Karla Kuskin. Reprinted by permission of Harper & Row, Publishers, Inc.

Excerpt from "De Koven" (and entire poem) from *Bronzeville Boys and Girls* by Gwendolyn Brooks. Copyright © 1956 by Gwendolyn Brooks, © renewed. Reprinted by permission of Harper & Row, Publishers, Inc.

Excerpt from "Picture People" from *Whispers and Other Poems* by Myra Cohn Livingston. Copyright © 1958 by Myra Cohn Livingston. Reprinted by permission of Marian Reiner for the author.

Rachel Isadora quote is reprinted from *Fifth Book of Junior Authors and Illustrators* (Bronx, NY: HW Wilson, 1983). All rights reserved. Reprinted by permission of the publisher.

Aliki Brandenberg quote from *Books for Your Children*, Birmingham, England, Spring 1984 issue. By permission of the publisher.

Excerpt from "Keep a Poem in Your Pocket" by Beatrice Schenk de Regniers. Copyright © 1958, 1986 by Beatrice Schenk de Regniers. By permission of the author.

"I Like You" by Masuhito appears in *I Like You*, selected and illustrated by Yaroslava. Copyright © 1976 Yaroslava Surmach Mills. Published by Charles Scribner's Sons.

(Acknowledgments continued on page 362.)

Cover Design: Barnett-Brandt Design
Cover Illustration: Don Daily

Copyright © 1990 Macmillan Publishing Company, a division of Macmillan, Inc.

Macmillan Publishing Company
866 Third Avenue
New York, N.Y. 10022
Collier Macmillan Canada, Inc.

Printed in the United States of America

ISBN: 0-02-243503-4

20 19 18 17 16 15 14 13 12

MACMILLAN
LANGUAGE ARTS TODAY

C O N T E N T S

THEME: *HERE AND THERE*

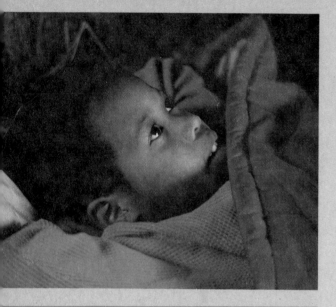

Language Study

Writing

AWARD WINNING
SELECTION

THEME: *GOOD DAYS*

Language Study

Writing

AWARD WINNING
SELECTION

Language Study

Writing

AWARD WINNING
SELECTION

THEME: *WISHES*

AWARD WINNING
SELECTION

THEME: *NEW WORLDS*

AWARD WINNING
SELECTION

WRITER'S REFERENCE

WRITER TO WRITER

I'm here to answer some questions about writing.

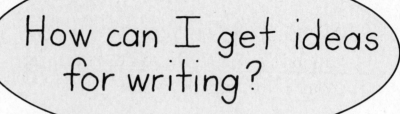

How can I get ideas for writing?

This book can help you. It is filled with great stories and poems by super writers. Each one I read makes me feel like writing.

Writers are readers, and readers are writers!

Sometimes I can't think of anything to write about. Then, I look at the **PICTURES** 📷 *SEEING LIKE A WRITER* section of this book. Wow! Soon I'm zooming away with lots of ideas.

What will I write about today?

IMAGINE

Writers look carefully. Careful lookers find ideas for writing.

How will I remember my ideas?

October 10

Grandpa's farm is great! I am glad to be here.

October 11

The pony is dark brown. How I wish it was mine!

JOURNAL My journal helps me remember all my ideas. I write in it every day. Sometimes I draw pictures, too.

A journal is a writer's best friend.

xiv

This report is good, but you forgot to give your opinion.

Thanks for helping me.

How does working with others help?

I like group writing. My classmates and I share ideas and write together. Soon, we are ready to write by ourselves.

Writing together helps writers get ideas

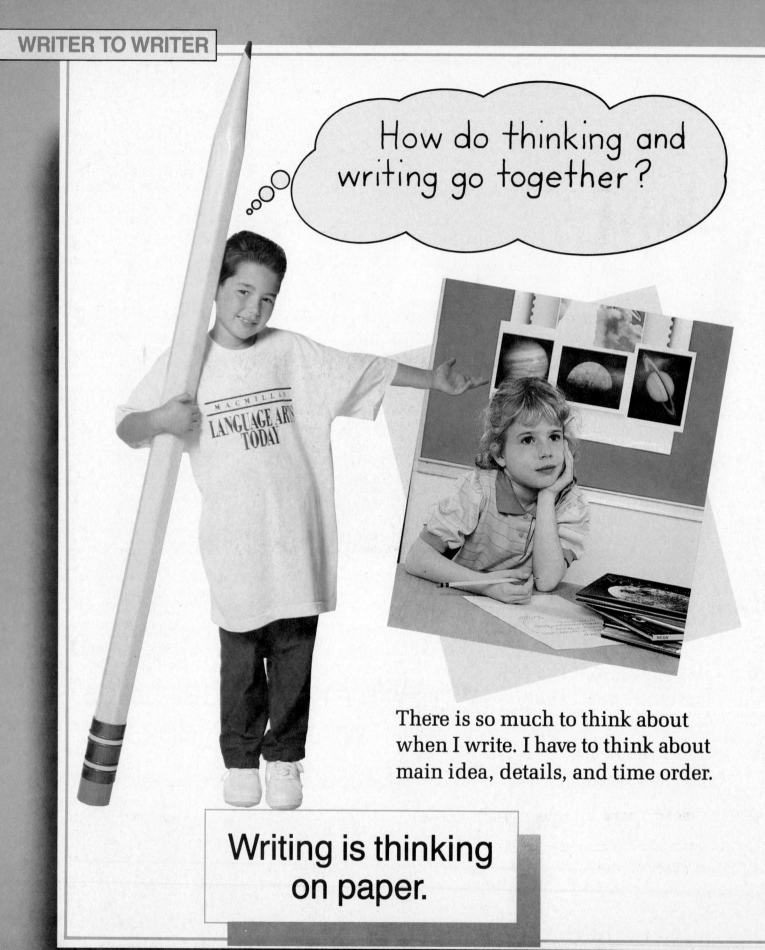

How do thinking and writing go together?

There is so much to think about when I write. I have to think about main idea, details, and time order.

Writing is thinking on paper.

What is the writing process? How will it help me?

Prewrite

I pick a topic for my purpose and audience.

bought him with my sister

Alf — eats all day

barks

Write a First Draft

I use my ideas to write a draft.

Revise

I take **TIME-OUT** to talk about my draft with a friend. Then I make changes in my draft.

Proofread

I fix all my mistakes in grammar, capitalization, and punctuation.

Publish

I make a clean copy of my draft. Then, I share it with my audience.

MACMILLAN

LANGUAGE ARTS TODAY

UNIT

1

Sentences

JOURNAL

Under the dark is a star,
Under the star is a tree,
Under the tree is a blanket,
And under the blanket is me.
Marchette Chute

1 GOOD LISTENERS AND SPEAKERS

When you talk with others, you take turns listening and speaking.

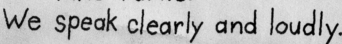

Cc Dd Ee Ff Gg Hh Ii Jj Kk Ll

We are good listeners and speakers.
We listen carefully.
We ask questions if we do not understand.
We think before we speak.
We take turns.
We speak clearly and loudly.

Why should you take turns?
Have a class discussion. Take turns talking about the first day of school. Remember to use the rules for listening and speaking.
Extra Practice, page 23

WRITING APPLICATION A Sentence

COOPERATIVE LEARNING

Write a sentence about how to make your classroom a better place for listening. Talk about your sentence with the class.

MECHANICS: Beginning and Ending Sentences

Every sentence must begin with a capital letter.

Our class took a trip.

Different types of sentences end with different end marks. Tell how each sentence ends.

CITY-HALL

Example	Type of Sentence	End Mark
I went on a trip.	statement	period (.)
When did you go?	question	question mark (?)
Tell me what you saw.	command	period (.)
What a great trip!	exclamation	exclamation mark (!)

 Tell how to begin and end each sentence.

Example: do you see the city hall   D   ?

1. the city hall is by the river
2. how beautiful it is
3. do you want to see the mayor
4. come inside with me

REMEMBER

- Begin every sentence with a capital letter.
- End different types of sentences with different end marks.

Mayor Maria Ruiz

 Write each sentence correctly.

Example: who works here   *Who works here?*

5. the mayor works here

6. will she speak today

7. listen to what she says

8. this is so interesting

9. may I ask a question

Extra Practice, page 27

COOPERATIVE LEARNING

WRITING APPLICATION A Class Story

Write a class story about a trip to a city hall. Use four different types of sentences. Begin and end each sentence correctly.

MECHANICS: Beginning and Ending Sentences   Have the children identify each type of sentence in the story.

8 VOCABULARY BUILDING: Words About Places

You can use sentences to tell about places.

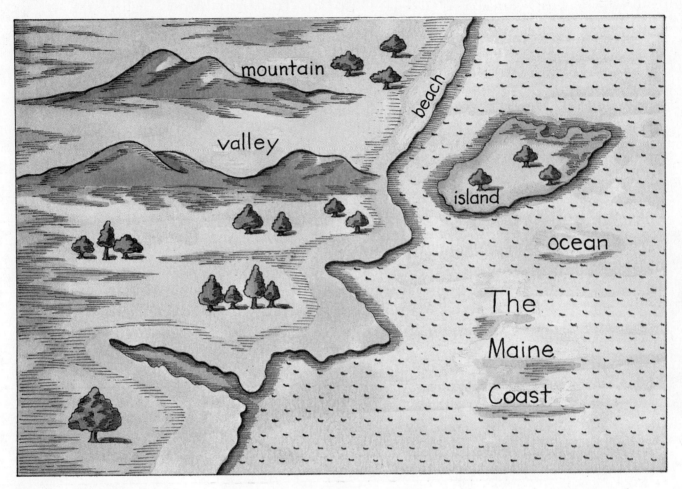

Find the ocean, beach, island, mountain, and valley on the map.

 Name the word in each sentence that tells about a place.

Example: A bird flies over the island.
   island

1. I like to see the waves in the ocean. ocean
2. Do you like to take walks on the beach? beach
3. This island is very small. island
4. There are pretty flowers in the valley. Valley
5. Let's climb to the top of the mountain. Mountain

REMEMBER

■ The words **beach**, **island**, **mountain**, **ocean**, and **valley** name places.

 Choose the word that correctly completes each sentence. Write the sentence.

Example: There are many fish in the (mountain, ocean).
There are many fish in the ocean.

6. I take a boat to the (valley, island).

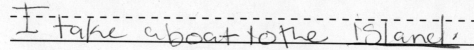
I take a boat to the Island.

7. I swim in the warm (ocean, beach).

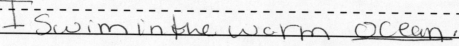
I swim in the warm ocean.

8. I find shells on the (valley, beach).

I find shells on the beach.

9. I climb the (ocean, mountain).

I climb the mountain.

10. The (valley, mountain) dips down.

The Valley dips down.

Extra Practice, page 27

WRITING APPLICATION Sentences

Write a few sentences about a trip you would like to take. Underline all the words in your story that name a place.

VOCABULARY: Words About Places   Have the children compile a class list of names of places.

GRAMMAR AND WRITING CONNECTION

Making Sentences Complete

A sentence must have a subject and predicate to be complete.

Joe and Kate build a sand castle.

This sentence is complete. Whom does the sentence tell about? What do they do?

COOPERATIVE LEARNING

With your classmates tell which group of words makes a sentence.

Example: I dig in the sand.   *sentence*

1. Ben jumps in the waves. *Sentence*
2. Sally and I. *no*
3. We walk on the beach. *Sentence*
4. floats on her back. *no*

Write each group of words that makes a sentence.

Example: The ocean is warm.   *The ocean is warm.*
            go every day.

5. I love the beach.
     The rocky shore.

I love the beach

6. sets up an umbrella.
     Did you bring a swimsuit?

Did you bring a swimsuit

7. The water is cold!
     Swimmers in the water.

The water is cold!

8. plays in the waves.
     Dry off with this towel.

 _Dry off with a this towel_

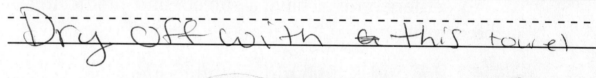

Read this story starter. Then use complete sentences to finish the story.

Rick fell asleep on the bus on the way home from school. When he finally woke up, he found himself in a very strange place.

GRAMMAR AND WRITING CONNECTION: Making Sentences Complete

UNIT CHECKUP

LESSON 1

Good Listeners and Speakers (page 2) Read each sentence. Is the child a good listener and speaker? Write **yes** or **no**.

1. Ellie listens carefully. _yes_

2. Bert never asks questions. _no / yes_

3. Dee speaks before she thinks. _no_

LESSON 2

Statements and Questions (page 3)   Read each sentence. Draw one line under each statement. Circle each question.

4. (What) do you do in your neighborhood?

5. I play ball in the park.

6. (Do you ever put on plays?)

LESSON 3

Commands (page 5)   Read each pair of sentences. Circle each command.

7. The bus is coming. (Wait for the bus.)

8. (Please do not push.) It is crowded.

9. (Pay the bus driver.) What is the cost?

LESSON 4

Exclamations (page 7)   Read each pair of sentences. Circle the exclamation.

10. We go to town. (What a long ride it is!)

11. Look at the cars. (How many there are!)

12. (How hungry I am!) May we eat lunch?

UNIT CHECKUP

Word Order in Sentences (page 9) Write each group of words to make a sentence.

13. flowers? you Do smell the

Do you smell the flowers?

14. the at clouds. Look

Look at the clouds.

15. little sees stream. Jed a

Jed sees a little stream.

LESSON 6

Parts of a Sentence (page 11) Draw one line under the subject. Draw two lines under the predicate.

16. I see the airplanes.
17. A man puts gas into one plane.
18. The suitcases are piled on a truck.

LESSON 7

Mechanics: Beginning and Ending Sentences (page 13) Circle the mark that completes each sentence.

19. How busy the city hall is ! .
20. Do you want to work there . ?
21. I want to be the mayor someday ? .

LESSON 8

Vocabulary Building: Words About Places (page 15) Circle the word in ( ) that completes each sentence.

22. Ned swims in the (valley, ocean).
23. He walks along the sandy (beach, mountain).
24. One day he will climb a (mountain, island).

LET'S GO!

Punctuation tells you how to read a sentence. For example, an exclamation mark tells you to read in an excited way. Fill in the line below with a place you love to go. Then, practice reading the parts with a partner.

Adam: I love to go to _____.
Will you come with me today?
Angie: I am not sure I can go.
Adam: It is a lot of fun!
Angie: Really? I will go with you.
Adam: That is great! Meet me here.

MY PLACE

Work with a partner. Each of you should think of your favorite place without writing down its name. Then, write three sentences that tell about the place. Next, write a question that asks where the place is. Exchange papers with your partner. Try to guess your partner's favorite place.

CREATIVE EXPRESSION

Read this poem.
Which actions can you feel?

MERRY-GO-ROUND

I climbed up on the
    merry-go-round,
And it went round
    and round.
I climbed up on a
    big brown horse,
and it went up
    and down.
Around and round
And up and down,
Around and round
And up and down.

—Dorothy W. Baruch

TRY IT OUT!

JOURNAL

Some poems repeat words or lines. You can almost hear and feel what the poem is about.

Imagine that you are on a ride in a park. Write a poem about it. Repeat words or lines to show the action.

EXTRA PRACTICE

Good Listeners and Speakers (page 2)   Read each sentence. Circle each rule for listening and speaking correctly.

1. Do not speak loudly.
2. Think before you speak.
3. Do not talk while others are talking.

Statements and Questions (page 3)   Read each sentence. Draw a line under each statement. Circle each question.

4. I am new here.
5. Where is the store?
6. Will you help me find it?

Commands (page 5)   Read each sentence. Circle each command.

7. The subway is crowded.
8. Give Grandma your seat.
9. Hold the pole tightly.

Exclamations (page 7)   Read each sentence. Circle each exclamation.

10. What a busy store!
11. How heavy the bag is!
12. Our friends shop, too.

Word Order in Sentences (page 9)   Write each group of words to make a sentence.

13.   birds? you feed Do the

_____

- -

_____

14.   the nest. in are They

_____

- -

_____

15.   into the John fell stream!

_____

- -

_____

16.   him? you Can help

_____

- -

_____

17.   will We try.

_____

- -

_____

18.   cold. The feels water

_____

- -

_____

19.   see I a turtle.

_____

- -

_____

20.   at Look fish! the

_____

- -

_____

Parts of a Sentence (page 11)   Draw one
line under the subject part. Draw two lines
under the predicate part.

21.   We went to the airport.

22.   Three airplanes landed at noon.

23.   Many people got off each airplane.

24.   Papa held my hand.

25.   The airport was filled with people.

26.   Two men carried our bags.

Additional practice for a difficult skill
Parts of a Sentence (page 11)

A. Complete each sentence with a subject part or
a predicate part. Use the sentence parts
in the box.

Dad	leaves the plane
The airplane	runs to his father

27. _____ lands softly.

28. Everyone _____ .

29. Brian _____ .

30. _____ gives Brian a hug.

GRAMMAR

B. Match each subject part with a predicate part to make a new sentence. Then write the sentence.

31.	Our class	zooms above us.
32.	The runway	flies her plane.
33.	An airplane	visits an airport.
34.	A pilot	is long.

31. _____

_____

32. _____

_____

33. _____

_____

34. _____

_____

Mechanics: Beginning and Ending Sentences

(page 13)   Circle the mark that completes each sentence.

35.   Please show me the map   ?   .
36.   Where is the city hall   !   ?
37.   What a fine building it is   !   .
38.   May we go inside   .   ?
39.   I will follow you   .   !

Vocabulary Building: Words About Places

(page 15)   Circle the word in ( ) that completes each sentence.

40.   We live on that (island, mountain) in the ocean.
41.   There is white sand on the (beach, ocean).
42.   The (valley, ocean) is cold and blue.
43.   The (valley, mountain) is low.
44.   Bob climbs the (ocean, mountain).
45.   Jan sees fish in the (valley, ocean).

GRAMMAR

UNIT 2

Writing Sentences

*I like to peek
inside a book
where all the picture people look.*
Myra Cohn Livingston

Have you ever used paper and markers to tell stories about places here and there? Bidemmi uses words and pictures to tell stories. Read to see what story Bidemmi tells.

CHERRIES
AND
CHERRY PITS

by Vera B. Williams

Bidemmi lives on the floor above me. We visit back and forth a lot. Bidemmi loves to draw, so when she opens the door I'm often standing there with a marker of some kind or color she doesn't have yet.

She always tries a new marker right away. First she makes a dot on the paper. Then she draws a line out from that dot. As she draws, she tells the story of what she is drawing. She always starts with the word THIS. THIS is the door to the subway . . .

• • •

THIS is me. And THIS is my station. I have to walk up the stairs one at a time so the bright sun that is out here in the sky won't make my eyes hurt. But right here on the street, what do you think there is going to be? A man is selling cherries from the back of his truck. His whole truck is going to be cherries. Nothing but cherries.

Now see this little purse? I have a little purse in my pocket with some money Mama gave me. When I show it to the man, he puts a bag on the scale and puts in some cherries. But then he goes ahead and fills it right up to the top and gives it to me.

"Don't eat them up too fast," he tells me.

Now what does that man think? I wasn't going to eat them up fast because I had an important plan. I walk home eating the cherries one by one and saving the pits, eating a cherry and saving the pit. I put every one of the pits in my pocket.

Notice how Bidemmi begins and ends each sentence in her story.

When I get to my street I take them all out. I kneel right down and I poke one in the ground on the edge of our yard. Our yard is a junky old yard. It has this stump where there used to be a tree. But that tree died and they came and cut it down and took it away.

Then I poke pits in the ground all over the place. I know if I plant enough of them at least one will grow. I pat the ground smooth.

I pour some water on each pit. And I tell those pits to grow . . . grow and grow.

•   •   •

Then one day I come out and the cherries are ripe. There are so many cherries, the branches reach right down to the ground. There are red cherries and dark red cherries and cherries such a deep red they are almost black.

Then the people come out the back door and the front door and down the steps. There are enough cherries for every single one of them. And even for their friends from Nairobi and Brooklyn, Toronto and St. Paul, who come down in these airplanes.

How do Bidemmi's sentences help you "see" the cherries?

So here we all are standing in front of the airplanes, eating cherries and spitting out pits, eating cherries and spitting out pits till we all fall down from eating so many cherries and spitting out pits. And . . .

THIS cherry pit and THIS cherry pit and all the cherry pits start to grow until there is a whole forest of cherry trees right on our block.

Thinking Like a Reader

1. Think about the story Bidemmi made up to go with her picture. What part of the story did you like the best?
2. Have you ever imagined a story all by yourself? What was it about?

Write your answers in your journal.

Thinking Like a Writer

3. How does the author let you know that Bidemmi lives in the city?
4. If you were writing a story about a tree, where would your story take place?
5. How would you let your readers know about that place?

Write your ideas in your journal.

Brainstorm *Vocabulary*

Bidemmi tells about a subway and an airplane. Draw pictures of some other ways we travel. Write the word under each picture that names what you drew. Write any new words in a personal word list.

Talk It Over *Put Yourself in the Story*

Work with a partner. Imagine you are the people in Bidemmi's story. Imagine that you are eating some of the cherries she grew. Talk to each other about the cherries. Use statements, questions, commands, and exclamations as you talk.

Quick Write *Write Questions*

Imagine that you are a newspaper reporter who sees a forest of cherry trees growing on a city block. What questions would you ask? Write four questions on a sheet of paper.

Idea Corner *Think About Here and There*

Think of some ideas for your own sentences about a place. Make a list of places to write about. You might also draw a picture.

PICTURES  SEEING LIKE A WRITER

Finding Ideas for Writing

Look at the pictures. Think about what you see.
What ideas for writing sentences do the pictures give you?
Write your ideas in your journal.

1 GROUP WRITING: Sentences

COOPERATIVE
LEARNING

For what **purpose** might you write a sentence? You can use sentences to share your ideas. Your sentences must make sense for your **audience** to understand them. What makes a sentence make sense?

■ A Complete Thought
■ Correct Word Order

A Complete Thought

Every sentence tells a complete thought. The subject part tells who or what does something. The predicate part tells what that person or thing does or did.

Our class   sees new places.

Guided Practice: Matching Sentence Parts

Work with your class to match subjects and predicates to make sentences.

Everyone   tastes good.
The food   crawl toward the crumbs.
Little ants   stops for lunch.

Correct Word Order

When you write a sentence, put the words in the correct order.

big? the island Is   Is the island big?

Putting a Sentence Together

A chart can help you decide what to write about. Look at the chart that Brian made.

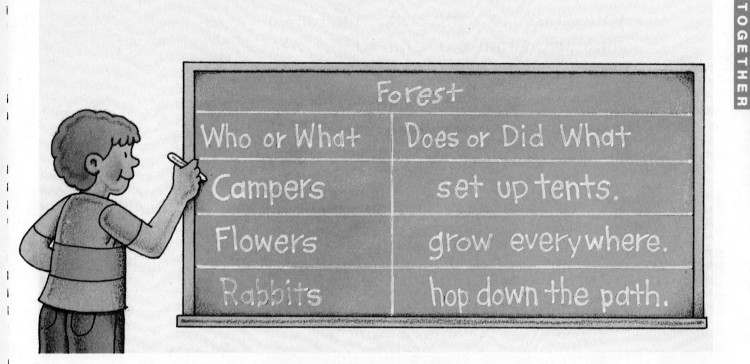

Forest	
Who or What	Does or Did What
Campers	set up tents.
Flowers	grow everywhere.
Rabbits	hop down the path.

Guided Practice: Writing Sentences

Choose a favorite place. Make a chart like the one Brian made. Then write complete sentences about your place.

Checklist: Sentences

A checklist can help you to remember important points for writing sentences. Complete this checklist.

CHECKLIST

- ✔ Purpose and audience
- ✔ A complete thought
- ✔ _____

When you want to write about something or someone, look at it carefully. Then you will be able to write clear, complete sentences about it.

Rita visited the ranch in the picture. She wanted to write about the ranch. She made a chart of the things she saw.

Rodeo Ranch	
Who or What	Does or Did What
A rancher	rides a horse.
The sheep	eat grass.

Thinking Like a Writer

- Look at the picture. What else might Rita want to add to her chart?
- What sentences might Rita write about Rodeo Ranch?

COOPERATIVE
LEARNING

Look at the picture. Then read the writer's chart. Talk with a classmate and match each person with an action. Then rewrite the chart correctly on another piece of paper. Add one more observation to the chart.

Outside My Window	
Who or What	Does or Did What
Jose'	carries letters.
A man	walks five dogs.
A woman	feeds the birds.
Martina	skates.

WRITING

TOGETHER

3 INDEPENDENT WRITING: Sentences

Prewrite: Step 1

A sentence tells a complete thought. Its words are in the correct order.

Josh wanted to write about a place his classmates might want to visit. Here is how Josh chose a topic.

Choosing a Topic

First, Josh made a list of places he had visited.

Next, he closed his eyes and tried to picture each place.

Last, he decided on the place that he could remember best.

the pumpkin farm   This is
the aquarium   my favorite
State Forest ⟵———— place.
Washington, D.C.

Josh picked the State Forest. He made a drawing of the State Forest to get ideas for writing. Notice how he wrote the names of important things in the picture.

Exploring Ideas: Drawing Strategy

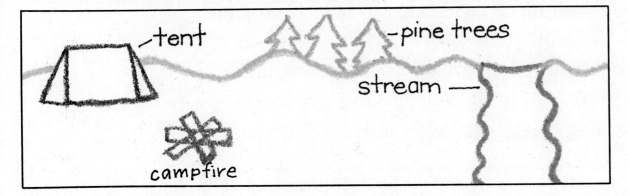

Josh thought about his **audience**, or who would read his sentences. He also thought about his **purpose**. Josh looked at his drawing again. He decided to add to it.

Thinking Like a Writer

■ What did Josh add to his drawing? Why?

YOUR TURN
JOURNAL

Think of a place that you would like to write about. Use **Pictures** or your journal for ideas. Follow these steps.

■ Make a list of places.
■ Choose the one you like the best.
■ Draw a picture of the place.
■ Think about your purpose and audience.

Write a First Draft: Step 2

Josh made a checklist to help him write his sentences correctly.

Here is Josh's draft.

you will like the state forest.

In a tent.

Guess what we saw.

hunted for acorns chipmunks.

A beaver family.

Beavers are in the zoo, too.

As Josh wrote, he did not worry about mistakes.

He knew that he could fix mistakes later.

YOUR TURN

Write your first draft. Be sure to write complete sentences that make sense. Ask yourself these questions.

- What will my audience want to know?
- How can I make my sentences interesting?

🕐 **TIME-OUT** You might want to take some time out before you revise. Think about what you want to change.

Planning Checklist
- Remember purpose and audience.
- Write a complete thought.
- Use correct word order.

Revise: Step 3

After he finished his first draft, Josh read it over to himself. Then, he shared his writing with a classmate. He wanted ideas for making his sentences better.

Your sentences are pretty good, but you need to tell more.

OK, I'll do that. Thanks.

Josh looked back at his planning checklist to make sure his sentences were complete. He put a check next to the step that he forgot. He now has a checklist to use as he revises.

Revising Checklist
- Remember purpose and audience.
- ✔ Write a complete thought.
- Use correct word order.

Josh made changes to his sentences. He did not correct small mistakes. He knew he could fix them later.

Here are Josh's revised sentences.

you will like the state forest.
~~My family lived~~
In a tent.
~~It was a big, green tent.~~
Guess what we saw.
hunted for acorns chipmunks.
played in the water.
A beaver family.

Beavers are in the zoo, too.

Thinking Like a Writer

- In which sentence did he change the word order?
- Do you think Josh's changes made his sentences better? Why or why not?

YOUR TURN

Read your first draft. Ask yourself these questions.

- Do I need to add or take out a sentence?
- Is each sentence complete?
- Is my word order correct?

Proofread: Step 4

Josh knew he had to proofread his sentences before he was really finished. He used this proofreading checklist.

Here is part of Josh's proofread sentences.

> you will like the state forest.
> ≡My family lived
> In a tent.
>   It was a big, green tent.
> Guess what we saw.?

YOUR TURN

Proofreading Practice

Proofread these sentences. Use proofreading marks to correct the mistakes.

Where did we go.

we went to the desert?

flowers were blooming everywhere!

Proofreading Checklist
- Did I use capital letters correctly?
- Did I use the correct end marks?

Applying Your Proofreading Skills

Now proofread the sentences you wrote. Read your proofreading checklist. Review **The Grammar Connection** and **The Mechanics Connection**, too. Use proofreading marks to correct mistakes.

Proofreading Marks

∧ Add
− Take out
≡ Make a capital letter
/ Make a small letter

THE GRAMMAR CONNECTION

Remember these rules about sentences.
■ A **sentence** tells a complete thought.
■ The words in a sentence are in a logical order.
   My family hikes to the river.

THE MECHANICS CONNECTION

Remember these rules about punctuation.
■ A **statement** and a **command** end with a **period**.
   We sit on a big log.
   Look at all the fish.
■ An **exclamation** ends with an **exclamation mark**.
   How cold the water is!
■ A **question** ends with a **question mark**.
   May we go swimming?

Publish: Step 5

Josh wanted to share his sentences with his class. He copied his sentences in his best handwriting. Then Josh hung his paper on the board.

YOUR TURN

Make a final copy of your sentences for your classmates to read. Use your best handwriting. Here are some other ways to share your sentences.

SHARING SUGGESTIONS

Draw a picture of the place you wrote about on a big piece of paper. Write one of your sentences on the paper. Use it as a place mat.	Write each sentence on a strip of paper. Use the strips to make a place mobile. Add a picture to your mobile.	Make a picture post card of the place you visited. Write one or two of your sentences on the card.

4 SPEAKING AND LISTENING: Giving Directions

You can use what you know about writing complete sentences to give directions to your classmates.

First, pick something you know how to do or make. Next, draw the steps in order. Be sure to put in all of the steps.

How to Make a Bird Feeder

1.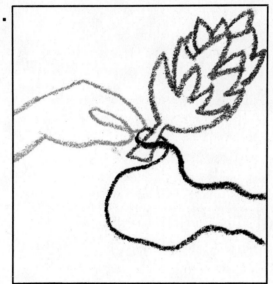

2.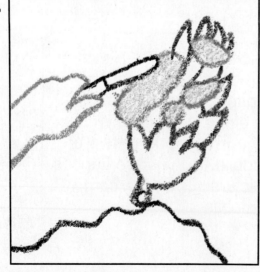

3.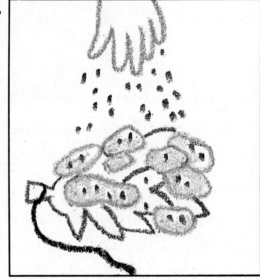

4.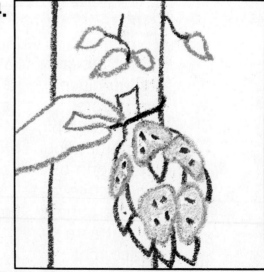

Use these guidelines for giving your directions.

SPEAKING GUIDELINES: Giving Directions

1. Draw pictures of the steps.
2. Speak loudly and clearly.
3. Tell about each step in the right order.
4. Ask listeners if they have questions.

■ How does telling the steps in order help my listeners?

■ Why should I ask my listeners if they have questions?

SPEAKING APPLICATION Giving Directions

Give directions to your classmates for making something to eat. First, make pictures of the steps. Then, use the speaking guidelines to help you talk. Your classmates will use the guidelines below as they listen.

LISTENING GUIDELINES: Giving Directions

1. Listen to all the steps.
2. Follow each step.
3. Ask questions if you do not understand.

5 WRITER'S RESOURCES: A Writer's Journal

In this unit, you wrote sentences about places. Keeping a **journal** can help you remember your thoughts about places, people, and things.

You can write about anything you wish in a journal. Do not worry about making mistakes when you write in your journal. Your journal is just for you to read. Use your journal to get ideas for your other writing.

Look at these journal notes that Jay wrote.

October 10

Grandpa's farm is great! I am glad to be here.

October 11

The pony is dark brown. How I wish it was mine!

 Read Jay's notes again. Then write two or three sentences about what you did or saw today.

WRITING APPLICATION A Journal

Try to write in your journal every day. Write the date at the top of each page. Write about those things you want to remember. Use your journal to find ideas for your other writing.

Writing About Social Studies

Social studies is about people and places all over the world. It is also about people and places of long ago.

ACTIVITIES

Picture a Place

Draw a picture of some homes you see in your neighborhood. Share your picture with your classmates.

Write About a Place

Write about the homes you drew. Write one sentence that tells how they are alike. Write another sentence that tells how they are different.

Respond to Literature

My Prairie Year by Brett Harvey is a book based on the journal of Elenore Plaisted (plā sted), a nine-year-old girl. In 1889, she moved to the Dakotas from Maine. Read about her new home. Then imagine you lived when Elenore did. Write a journal page that tells about your new home.

My Prairie Year

Our house on the prairie was like a little white ship at sea. Not a tree, not a bush to be seen—just endless tall grass that billowed in the wind like the waves of an ocean.

UNIT CHECKUP

LESSON 1
Group Writing: Sentences (page 38) Match sentence parts
to write three sentences.

A family	gets stuck in a tree.
The kite	eats bread crumbs.
A bird	has a picnic.

LESSON 2
Thinking: Observing (page 40) Study the picture. Then,
on a separate piece of paper, write three sentences about it.
Use a different subject in each sentence.

LESSON 3
Writing Sentences (page 42) Write a page in your journal
about a class trip that you would like to take.

LESSON 4
Speaking and Listening: Giving Directions (page 50)
Write three steps, in order, that you might use to
give directions to someone for making a puppet.

LESSON 5
A Writer's Journal (page 52) On another paper,
write three sentences that tell when you write in
your journal.

THEME PROJECT   TRAVEL POSTERS

You have practiced writing sentences about places. A travel poster tells about a place. It makes people want to visit that place.

Look at this travel poster. Talk with your classmates about how the poster makes people want to go to Dreamland.

Think of a place. Brainstorm ideas about the place.
■ Make a travel poster for that place.
■ Use pictures and sentences that will make others want to visit that place.

UNIT

3

Nouns

How do you like to go up in a swing,
Up in the air so blue?
Oh, I do think it the pleasantest thing
Ever a child can do!

Robert Louis Stevenson
from "The Swing"

1 WHAT IS A NOUN?

A noun names a person, place, or thing.

The **girl** sees a **rabbit** in the **park**.

The words **girl**, **rabbit**, and **park** are nouns. What does each noun name?

 Read each sentence. Then circle the noun.

Example: A raccoon hides.

(raccoon)

1. My brother hikes.

2. This mountain is high!

3. The trail is long.

Finish each sentence with a noun from the box.

Example: My ___ is heavy. | hat pack | *My pack is heavy.*

| breeze   bird   sun |

4. A red ___bird___ sings.

5. The ___sun___ shines brightly.

6. The ___breeze___ is cool.

Extra Practice, page 79

WRITING APPLICATION A Picture and a Sentence

Imagine that you are on a hike. Draw a picture of a person, place, or thing you see on your hike. Write a sentence about the picture. Then circle the noun.

2 NOUNS FOR PEOPLE

You know that a noun names a **person**.
What are some nouns you know that name
a person?

The **girl** plays a drum.
Her **father** takes a picture.

Which nouns name people?

Read each sentence. Then write the noun that names
a person.

Example: My mother is in the parade.   mother

1. A clown blows a horn.   *clown*

2. My brother rides a horse.   *brother*

3. The dancer kicks her legs.   *dancer*

4. A baby waves a blue flag.   *baby*

5. The tall man tips his hat.   *man*

Extra Practice, page 79

COOPERATIVE
LEARNING

WRITING APPLICATION A Class Story

Write a class story about the people in a parade.
Circle the nouns that name people.

GRAMMAR

3 NOUNS FOR PLACES AND THINGS

A noun can name a **place** or a **thing**.

We take the **bus** to the **museum**.

Which noun names a thing?   Which noun names a place?

 Write each sentence. Circle the noun that names a thing.
Draw a line under the noun that names a place.

Example: We pass a bench in the hall.

We pass a (bench) in the hall.

1. We read a sign in the room.

_____

2. I see a deer by the forest.

_____

3. A fire burns in the village.

_____

4. A fish swims in the river.

_____

5. A boat is near the shore.

_____

Extra Practice, page 79

WRITING APPLICATION A Story

Write a story about a visit to a museum. Tell about
the things you saw at the museum.

4 SPECIAL NOUNS FOR PEOPLE, PETS, AND PLACES

Some nouns name special people, pets, and places. Special nouns begin with **capital letters**.

Nouns	Special Nouns
boy	Ed
cat	Fluffy
street	Jones Street or Jones St.
city	Fernwood

Which capital letters do you use to write your name?

 Tell which nouns need capital letters.

Example: Will jan go to the pet show?   *Jan*

1. My friend tim goes to the show.
2. He is taking his cat named socks.
3. He lives on main st.
4. The show is in hillsdale.

REMEMBER

■ The names of special people, pets, and places begin with **capital letters**.

Write each sentence correctly.

Example: Will your cat slinky
win a prize?
*Will your cat Slinky
win a prize?*

5. I see hoppy at the pet show.

- -

6. Will bob bring his dog?

- -

7. The show is in kentland.

- -

8. It will be on west st.

- -

9. My sister peg will be there.

- -

Extra Practice, page 79

WRITING APPLICATION A Poster

Work with your class to make a pet show poster. Write the name of the person who will judge the show. Then, list the names of the pets who will be in the show. Last, write where the show will be.

GRAMMAR: Special Nouns for People, Pets, and Places · Bring to the children's attention the abbreviated form for *street.* Note the capitalization and punctuation.

5 DAYS, MONTHS, AND HOLIDAYS

Nouns that name days, months, and holidays begin with **capital letters**.

Days of the Week	Months of the Year		Holidays
Monday	January	July	Martin Luther King Day
Tuesday	February	August	Groundhog Day
Wednesday	March	September	Thanksgiving
Thursday	April	October	
Friday	May	November	
Saturday	June	December	
Sunday			

What day is today? What is the month?

 Tell which nouns need a capital letter.

Example: I train for the team in march.   *March*

1. Our team plays ball in april.
2. The big game is next saturday.
3. We are practicing on thursday.
4. Our last game is after memorial day.

REMEMBER

- Nouns that name days, months, and holidays begin with **capital letters**.

 Write each sentence correctly.

Example: We went to the game on father's day.
We went to the game on Father's Day.

5. I joined the team in june.

- -

6. We will play on friday.

- -

7. I bought a new glove on monday.

- -

8. I got a bat in july.

- -

9. I play on independence day.

- -

10. One game is in august.

- -

Extra Practice, page 80

WRITING APPLICATION A Story

Imagine that you are on a famous ball team. Write a story about a big holiday game. Use nouns that name days, months, and the holiday.

Remind the children that each important word in the name of a holiday begins with a capital letter.

6 MORE THAN ONE

A noun can also name more than one.

- Add **s** to most nouns to name more than one.

  tool   tool**s**

- Add **es** to nouns that end with **s**, **ss**, **ch**, **sh**, and **x**.

  bus bus**es**   dress dress**es**
  ranch ranch**es**   bush bush**es**
  fox fox**es**

Read the nouns above.

Which nouns mean more than one?

 Tell how to change each noun in ( ) to name more than one.

Example: Our two (class) work hard.   *classes*

1. We make (plan) for a clubhouse.
2. We will use (branch) for the roof.
3. I can make a table out of (box).
4. Tina will make some (chair).
5. Dick will buy (dish).

REMEMBER

- Add **s** to most nouns to name **more than one**.
- Add **es** to nouns that end with **s**, **ss**, **ch**, **sh**, and **x**.

Make the noun in ( ) name more than one. Then write the new sentence.

Example: Two (bus) pass us as we work.
Two buses pass us as we work.

6. We make our clubhouse with (box).

----

7. We need more (nail).

----

8. Paint with these (brush).

----

9. Here comes Al with (glass) of juice.

----

10. My (friend) show him the house.

Extra Practice, Practice Plus, pages 80-81

WRITING APPLICATION A Plan

Plan a clubhouse with your class. Write about the things you will use to build it.

Have the children tell how they made each noun plural.

7 MORE WORDS FOR MORE THAN ONE

Some nouns change their spelling to name more than one.

man ←→ men   foot ←→ feet   child ←→ children
woman ←→ women   tooth ←→ teeth   mouse ←→ mice

Which nouns name more than one?

 Make the noun in (   ) name more than one. Then write the new sentence.

Example: Many (child) like farms. *Many children like farms.*

1. Two (man) stack the hay.

- -

2. Four (woman) feed the horses.

- -

3. What big (tooth) the horses have!

- -

4. Three (mouse) run across the barn.

- -

5. They run on tiny (foot).

- -

Extra Practice, page 82

 WRITING APPLICATION A Story

Write a story about a day in the barn.

8 MECHANICS: Titles and Dates

Titles and dates also begin with capital letters.

Use a period after **Mrs.**, **Ms.**, **Mr.**, and **Dr.**
Miss does not end with a period.

Begin a month with a capital letter.
Put a comma between the day and year in
a date.   May 14, 1990

How would you write today's date?

 Write each sentence correctly.

Example: Will mrs Barton help us?
                Will Mrs. Barton help us?

1. Our fair is on may 14 1990.

_____

2. I hope ms Wong will bake rolls.

_____

3. Will dr Lopez sell some plants?

_____

4. I sent invitations on april 3 1990.

_____

Extra Practice, page 83

COOPERATIVE
LEARNING

WRITING APPLICATION A Class Plan

Plan a fair with your class. Write a few sentences that
tell when the fair will be and who will help you.

VOCABULARY BUILDING:
Compound Words

A **compound word** is made from two words.

blue + bird = bluebird

Which two words make up **bluebird**?

rain + bow = rainbow

 Name the compound word in each sentence.
Tell which words make up the compound.

Example: The doghouse is new.

doghouse   dog + house

1. I feel the bright sunlight.
2. Mom looks at a rainbow.
3. Eric finds a butterfly.
4. Nina tastes a blueberry.
5. A goldfish swims in the pool.

REMEMBER

■ A **compound word** is made from two words.

Match the words to make compound words.

sun————crow
back————flower
grass   yard
scare   hopper

Complete each sentence with a compound word you made. Write each sentence.

6. We have a garden in the ___.

- -

7. A yellow ___ grows there.

- -

8. I see a ___ under a bush.

- -

9. A funny ___ stands in our garden.

- -

Extra Practice, page 83

WRITING APPLICATION Vocabulary and Writing

Work together. Write a story about a scarecrow's birthday party in the garden. Circle any compound words that you used.

GRAMMAR AND WRITING CONNECTION

Using Nouns in Sentences

Use exact nouns to tell more about what you think or feel. Exact nouns make your sentences clear and interesting.

Which sentence tells you more?

Sam likes to go to a **place**.
Sam likes to go to a **zoo**.

The second sentence tells you more. It gives you a clearer picture of where Sam likes to go.

COOPERATIVE
LEARNING

With your classmates read the nouns in the chart. Under each noun list a more exact one.

animal	building	clothes	food
bear			

Bob wrote these sentences about the zoo. Help Bob decide which noun to use in each sentence.

 Choose the more exact noun. Write the new sentence.

Example: A (woman, person) fed the ducks.
A woman fed the ducks.

1. We stood around a big (thing, cage).

- -

2. The huge (animal, lion) roared.

- -

3. The seals played with a (toy, ball).

- -

4. The hippo stood in the (water, pond).

- -

5. A giraffe ate (food, hay).

- -

Imagine that you are an animal in the zoo. What kind of animal are you? Write a story about your day. Be sure to use exact nouns to make your sentences interesting.

UNIT CHECKUP

LESSON
1

What Is a Noun? (page 60)   Read each sentence. Then circle the noun in each sentence.

1. The forest is cool.
2. A hiker walks softly.
3. The stream is cold.

LESSON
2

Nouns for People (page 61)   Read each sentence. Then circle the noun that names a person.

4. My brother is in the parade.
5. Your friend is playing a tuba.
6. That girl is riding a bike.

LESSON
3

Nouns for Places and Things (page 62)   Read each sentence. Circle each noun that names a thing. Draw a line under each noun that names a place.

7. Open the door of the museum.
8. Look at that picture in the hall.
9. That room has a dinosaur in it.

LESSON
4

Special Nouns for People, Pets, and Places (page 63)
Write each sentence correctly.

10. The show is in new york.

- -

11. It is on fern street.

- -

12. Will barry come?

- -

UNIT CHECKUP

LESSON **5**

Days, Months, and Holidays (page 65)
Circle each sentence that is written correctly.

13. We play ball in october.
14. We practice every Tuesday.
15. Our next game is on Halloween.

LESSON **6**

More Than One (page 67) Circle each noun that names more than one.

16. boxes box
17. class classes
18. bench benches
19. dishes dish

LESSON **7**

More Words for More Than One (page 69)
Circle each noun that names more than one.

20. men man
21. tooth teeth
22. mice mouse
23. children child

LESSON **8**

Mechanics: Titles and Dates (page 70)
Circle each sentence that is written correctly.

24. Our fair is on October 18, 1990.
25. I hope dr Dobbs will come.
26. Please ask Miss Abrams to help decorate.

LESSON **9**

Vocabulary Building: Compound Words (page 71) Match the words to make compound words.

27. ▪ grape ▪ rise
28. ▪ sun ▪ fruit

SENTENCE STRETCH

Play this with a partner. Look at this sentence and think of things you might see at a parade.

I went to a parade and saw a _____.

Now take turns with your partner and add one noun after another to the sentence. Remember to repeat all the old nouns before adding a new noun of your own.

SHOPPING DAY

It is fun to go shopping. Copy the stores below on a separate piece of paper. Then make a shopping list. Write three nouns that name things you can buy in each store.

Bakery
Vegetable Stand
Clothing Store

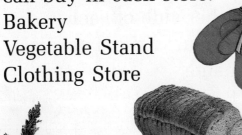

SPLISH SPLASH

What can you make with paper on a rainy day? Write a paragraph that tells how to make something. Write all the steps in order.

ADD IT

b5nch p24pl2 h44K

You can play this with one or more friends. First, write six nouns. Then, write this list on your paper.

a = 1   **e** = 2   **i** = 3   **o** = 4   **u** = 5

Add the points for these letters in each noun. See who wrote the noun with the most points.

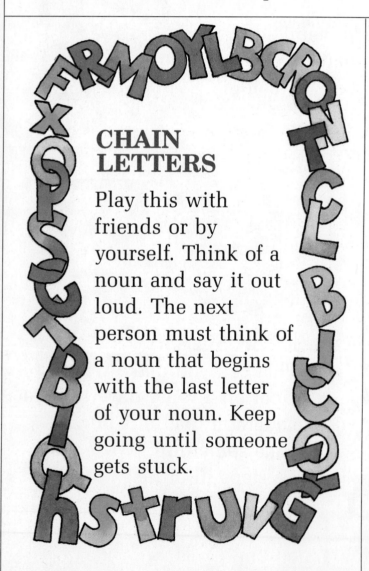

CHAIN LETTERS

Play this with friends or by yourself. Think of a noun and say it out loud. The next person must think of a noun that begins with the last letter of your noun. Keep going until someone gets stuck.

CUT IT OUT!

On white paper draw shapes for people and animals and cut them out. Write a noun on each cutout. On the other side of each cutout, write a special name.

EXTRA PRACTICE

What Is a Noun? (page 60)   Read each sentence.
Circle the word that is a noun.

1. A man hikes.
2. Each child follows.
3. The path is beautiful.

Nouns for People (page 61)   Circle each noun
that names a person.

4. The teacher leads the parade.
5. A girl claps her hands.
6. One boy taps his toes.

Nouns for Places and Things (page 62)   Read
each sentence. Circle the noun that names a
thing. Draw a line under the noun that names
a place.

7. I see a painting in the museum.
8. It shows a boat on a lake.
9. I go to the hall and sit on a bench.

Special Nouns for People, Pets, and Places
(page 63)   Circle the word that correctly completes
each sentence.

10. The pet show is on High (road, Road).
11. It is the best show in (Pratt, pratt).
12. My friend (Jay, jay) brings his dog.

Days, Months, and Holidays (page 65)
Write each underlined noun correctly.

13. Our team plays on <u>tuesday</u>.

- -

14. The weather in <u>june</u> is good.

- -

15. We won the game on <u>father's day</u>.

- -

16. Sometimes we play in <u>september</u>.

- -

17. The <u>labor day</u> game was exciting.

- -

More Than One (page 67)   Write each noun to name more than one.

18. club _____

19. box _____

20. wish _____

21. class _____

22. bench _____

Additional practice for a difficult skill
More Than One (page 67)
A. Circle the nouns that name more than one.

23. bush   **26.** fox

24. friends   **27.** matches

25. buses   **28.** kisses

B. Make the noun in ( ) name more than one. Then write the new sentence.

29. My family builds (thing).

- -

30. Dad and Mom pack (box).

- -

31. They make (bench).

- -

32. I put (dish) inside the house.

- -

33. Then I paint the (wall).

- -

More Words for More Than One (page 69)

Write each noun to name more than one.

34. foot

_____

- - - - - - - - - - - - -

_____

35. child

_____

- - - - - - - - - - - - -

_____

36. mouse

_____

- - - - - - - - - - - - -

_____

37. tooth

_____

- - - - - - - - - - - - -

_____

38. woman

_____

- - - - - - - - - - - - -

_____

39. man

_____

- - - - - - - - - - - - -

_____

Mechanics: Titles and Dates (page 70)

Write each sentence correctly.

40. The fair is on may 3 1989.

41. Will mrs Sanchez bake muffins?

42. I hope dr Harris can come.

43. The race is on july 17 1990.

44. They saw mr kahn run.

Vocabulary Building: Compound Words

(page 71)   Match the words to make compound words.

45.	air	house
46.	sail	plane
47.	foot	boat
48.	dog	ball
49.	wind	doors
50.	in	mill

UNIT

4

Writing a Paragraph

I see the way a child sees.
Rachel Isadora

AWARD
WINNING
SELECTION

Have you ever seen a dancing ball player?
Read about Max, who has fun wherever
he goes.

MAX

by Rachel Isadora

Notice how the
author presents
each story event
in time order.
What happens
first in the story?

Max is a great baseball player. He can run
fast, jump high, and hardly ever misses a
ball. Every Saturday he plays with his team
in the park.

On Saturday mornings he walks with his
sister Lisa to her dancing school. The school
is on the way to the park.

One Saturday when they reach the school
Max still has lots of time before the game is
to start. Lisa asks him if he wants to come
inside for a while.

Max does not really want to, but he says
O.K. Soon the class begins. He gets a chair
and sits near the door to watch.

The teacher invites Max to join the class, but he must take off his sneakers first.

He stretches at the barre. He tries to do the split. And the pas de chat. He is having fun.

Just as the class lines up to do leaps across the floor, Lisa points to the clock. It is time for Max to leave.

Max doesn't want to miss the leaps. He waits and takes his turn. Then he must go. He leaps all the way to the park.

He is late. Everybody is waiting for him. He goes up to bat.

Strike one!

He tries again.

Strike two!

And then . . .

A home run!

Now Max has a new way to warm up for the game on Saturdays. He goes to dancing class.

Thinking Like a Reader

1. In a few sentences, tell how Max feels about dancing.
2. How does dancing make you feel?

Write your answers in your journal.

Thinking Like a Writer

3. How does the author let you know how Max feels about dancing?
4. If you were writing a story about a fun activity, which one would you choose?
5. How would you let your readers know how much fun the activity is?

Write your ideas in your journal.

Brainstorm *Vocabulary*

Max enjoys baseball and ballet. Make a class list of things that you enjoy. Write the words in a personal word list. You can use words from your list when you write.

Talk It Over *Tell About a Picture*

Draw a picture of yourself having fun. Share your picture with a partner. Take turns telling about your pictures.

Quick Write *Write a Diary Page*

Write a diary page to tell about a day that was fun for you. Here is a diary page that Max might have written.

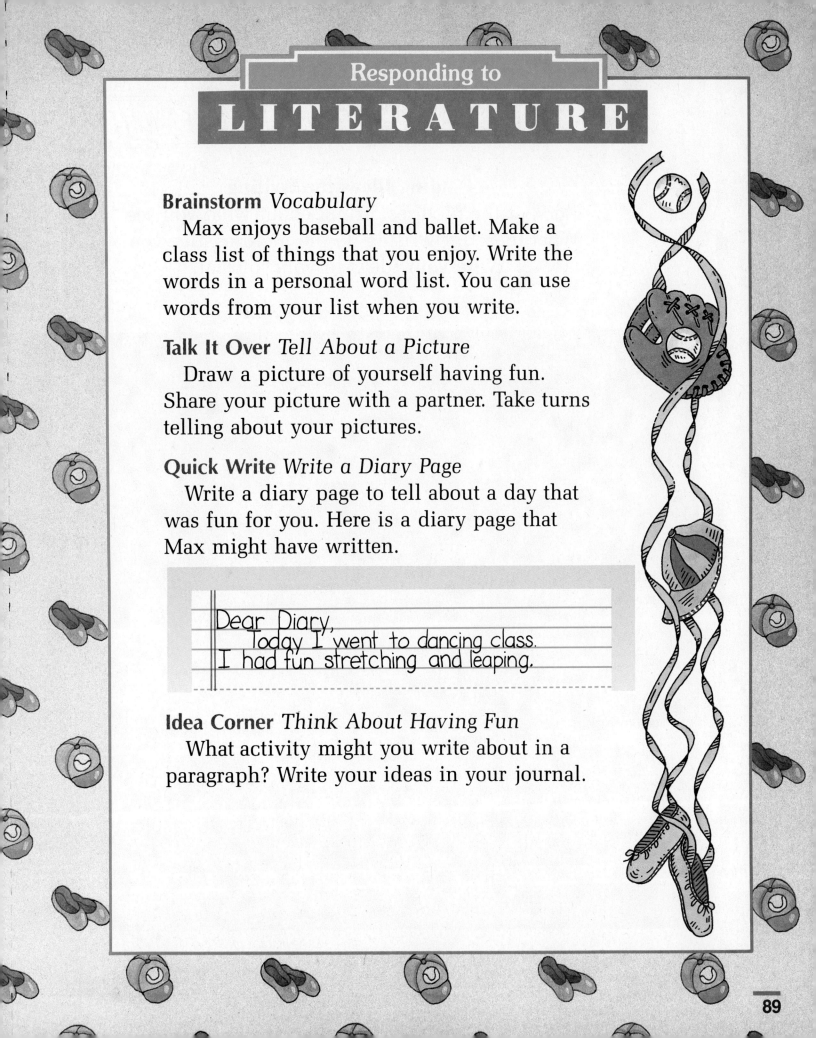

Dear Diary,
    Today I went to dancing class.
I had fun stretching and leaping.

Idea Corner *Think About Having Fun*

What activity might you write about in a paragraph? Write your ideas in your journal.

PICTURES SEEING LIKE A WRITER

Finding Ideas for Writing
Look at the pictures. Think about what you see.
What ideas for writing do the pictures give you?
Write your ideas in your journal.

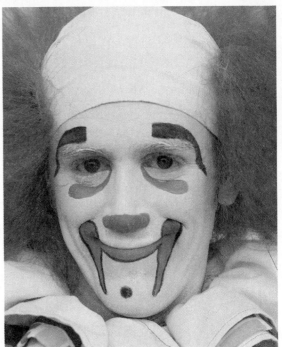

1 GROUP WRITING: A Narrative Paragraph

A paragraph is a group of sentences that tell about one main idea. When you write a narrative paragraph your **purpose** is to tell about something you did. Remember your **audience** when you write. What makes a narrative paragraph interesting?

- A Main-Idea Sentence
- Detail Sentences

A Main-Idea Sentence

Read the paragraph.

> I helped my team win the big game. I hit a home run. I also stole two bases. I even pitched for two innings. The coach was proud of me. I felt great!

The underlined sentence is the main-idea sentence. It tells the main idea of the paragraph.

The first sentence of a paragraph is always moved in, or indented.

Guided Practice:
Writing a Main-Idea Sentence

Talk about something fun your class has done. Write a main-idea sentence about it.

Detail Sentences

Detail sentences tell about the main idea. Use detail sentences in your paragraph.

Putting a Narrative Paragraph Together

A note card can help you choose details. Look at Maria's note card.

Details about the show
We sang songs. Jill played the piano. Taylor danced. Everyone clapped.

Guided Practice:

Writing a Narrative Paragraph

Look at your main-idea sentence. Then prepare a note card of details. Use your notes to write detail sentences.

Checklist: A Narrative Paragraph

Complete the checklist. Use it when you write a narrative paragraph.

CHECKLIST

✔ Purpose and audience
✔ Main-idea sentence

✔ _____

2 THINKING AND WRITING: Stating the Main Idea

Think about how to write a narrative paragraph. You know that all the sentences in a paragraph tell about the main idea.

You need to choose the main idea before you can write a paragraph. Sometimes thinking about details first can help you find the main idea.

Look at this page from Hector's journal.

January 10
We ate lunch in the playroom.
We played baseball with a rolled up sock.
Not one ant spoiled our fun.
I had fun at our winter picnic.

Hector used the details about his winter picnic to write a main-idea sentence.

THINKING AND WRITING: Stating the Main Idea

Thinking Like a Writer

■ Which sentence in Hector's journal do you think tells the main idea of the details?

The last sentence in Hector's journal tells the main idea. It tells what the other sentences are about.

When you write your paragraph, be sure to think of a main-idea sentence.

THINKING APPLICATION Stating the Main Idea

Read the detail sentences each writer wrote in a journal. Then circle the sentence that tells the main idea.

1. We saw dinosaur models. I bought two post cards. We met Kara at the museum.

    Our museum trip was wonderful.
    A museum is a big building.

2. I swam in the waves. Pete played in the sand. I found a pink shell.

    The beach is crowded in the summer.
    We will not forget our trip to the beach.

3. Our class saw the lions. We petted a fluffy sheep. I fed some monkeys.

    We had a great time at the zoo.
    Many people go to the zoo.

3 INDEPENDENT WRITING: A Narrative Paragraph

Prewrite: Step 1

Now you are ready to write your own narrative paragraph. First you must choose a topic. Here is how Lisa chose a topic.

Choosing a Topic

First, Lisa looked through her journal and made a list of fun things she had done.

Next, she thought about each one.

Last, she chose her favorite.

riding my bike
building a dog house
the pet show ← This was funny.

Lisa chose to write about a pet show. She explored her topic by making a chart.

Exploring Ideas: Charting Strategy

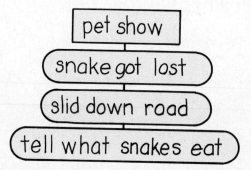

pet show
snake got lost
slid down road
tell what snakes eat

Lisa thought about her **audience**. She thought about her **purpose**. Lisa would tell her grandmother about the pet show.

Lisa made some changes in her chart.

Thinking Like a Writer

■ What changes did Lisa make? Why?

JOURNAL

Think of something fun you did to write about in a paragraph. Use **Pictures** or your journal for ideas. Follow these steps.

■ Make a list of things you did.
■ Choose the one you like best.
■ Make a chart of details.
■ Change your chart if necessary.
■ Think about your purpose and audience.

Write a First Draft: Step 2

Lisa made a checklist to help her write a first draft of her paragraph.

Here is Lisa's first draft.

Lisa did not worry about small mistakes. She would fix them later.

Al's pet Snake Slim got out of its cage. It slid down Bay road. My friend lives on that road. The man, mr. Lee, gave my pet a prize.

YOUR TURN

Planning Checklist
- Remember purpose and audience.
- Write a main-idea sentence.
- Write detail sentences that tell about the main idea.

Write your first draft. Write a main-idea sentence and detail sentences. Ask yourself these questions.

- What will my audience want to know?
- Do all my detail sentences tell about my main-idea sentence?

⏱ **TIME-OUT** You might want to take some time out before you revise. Think about what you want to change.

Revise: Step 3

After she finished her first draft, Lisa read it over to herself. Then, she shared her writing with a classmate. She wanted ideas for making her paragraph better.

Lisa looked at her planning checklist to make sure her paragraph was complete. She put a check next to the step that she forgot. She now has a checklist to use as she revises.

Revising Checklist
- ■ Remember purpose and audience.
- ■ Write a main-idea sentence.
- ✔ ■ Write detail sentences that tell about the main idea.

Lisa revised her paragraph. She did not fix small mistakes. She knew she could correct them later.

Our pet show was funny.
^Al's pet Snake Slim got out of its cage. It slid down Bay road.

My friend lives on that road. The
judge   dog Bif
man, mr. Lee, gave my pet a prize.
^

WISE
WORD
CHOICE

Thinking Like a Writer

- Which sentences did Lisa change?
- Do you think these changes made the paragraph better? Why?

YOUR TURN

Read your paragraph. Ask yourself these questions. Then revise your paragraph.

- Is my topic sentence clear?
- Do my detail sentences tell about the main idea?

Proofread: Step 4

Lisa knew her paragraph would not be complete until she proofread it. She used a proofreading checklist.

Here is part of Lisa's proofread paragraph.

> ~~Our pet show was funny.~~
> ∧Al's pet $\cancel{S}$nake Slim got out of its
> cage. It slid down Bay r̲o̲ad.
> My friend lives on that road. The
> ^judge^
> man, mr̲. Lee, gave my pet a prize.
> ∧   dog Bif

YOUR TURN

Proofreading Practice

Proofread this paragraph. Use proofreading marks to correct the mistakes.

> mrs Diego lets me do fun things in her pet shop. I can feed the mouses. Last monday I held two kittens

Proofreading Checklist
- Did I indent my paragraph?
- Did I use capital letters correctly?
- Did I use the correct end marks?

Applying Your Proofreading Skills

Now proofread your narrative paragraph. Read your checklist again. Review **The Grammar Connection** and **The Mechanics Connection**, too. Use the proofreading marks to correct your mistakes.

THE GRAMMAR CONNECTION

Remember these rules about nouns that name more than one person, place, or thing.
- Add **s** to most nouns to name more than one.
  turtle   turtle**s**
- Add **es** to nouns that end in **s**, **ss**, **ch**, **sh**, and **x**.
  leash   leash**es**
- Some nouns change their spelling to name more than one.
  child   child**ren**

THE MECHANICS CONNECTION

Remember these rules about writing special nouns.
- Special nouns for people, pets, and places begin with capital letters.
  Ms. **W**ong   **S**parky   **C**entral **R**oad
- The names of days, months, and holidays begin with capital letters.
  Monday   **J**une   **V**eteran's **D**ay

Proofreading Marks

∧ Add
— Take out
≡ Make a capital letter
/ Make a small letter

Publish: Step 5

Lisa wanted to share her narrative paragraph with her grandmother. She neatly copied her paragraph. Next, she drew a picture for the paragraph. Then, Lisa mailed everything to her grandmother.

YOUR TURN

Make a final copy of your narrative paragraph for your classmates to read. Use your best handwriting. Here are some other ways to share your paragraph.

SHARING SUGGESTIONS

With your classmates make a television news show to present your paragraphs.	Use your paragraph to make a picture book. Put a sentence on each page. Draw a picture for each sentence.	Act out the activity in your paragraph for your friends.

4 SPEAKING AND LISTENING: Making Introductions

You have written a narrative paragraph about something you did. You shared your happy time with others when you shared your paragraph. Introducing people to each other is another way to share your thoughts.

Read this introduction.

Follow these guidelines when you make an introduction.

SPEAKING GUIDELINES: Making Introductions

1. Introduce the younger person to the older person.
2. Say each person's name clearly.
3. Tell something about each person.

- Why should I say each person's name?
- How does my telling something about each person help them?

SPEAKING APPLICATION Making Introductions

Find two partners. Make up three people who like to do something fun. Write down some things you could tell about each person. Then act out an introduction for your class.

Use these guidelines as you listen to other children's introductions.

LISTENING GUIDELINES: Making Introductions

1. Listen to the name of the person that you are meeting.
2. Listen to what the speaker says about the person.
3. Say something polite to the new person.

5 WRITER'S RESOURCES: Maps

Maps help you find places. A map can also help you when you write about going someplace.

Jody is writing about a parade. She looks at a map of Greenport.

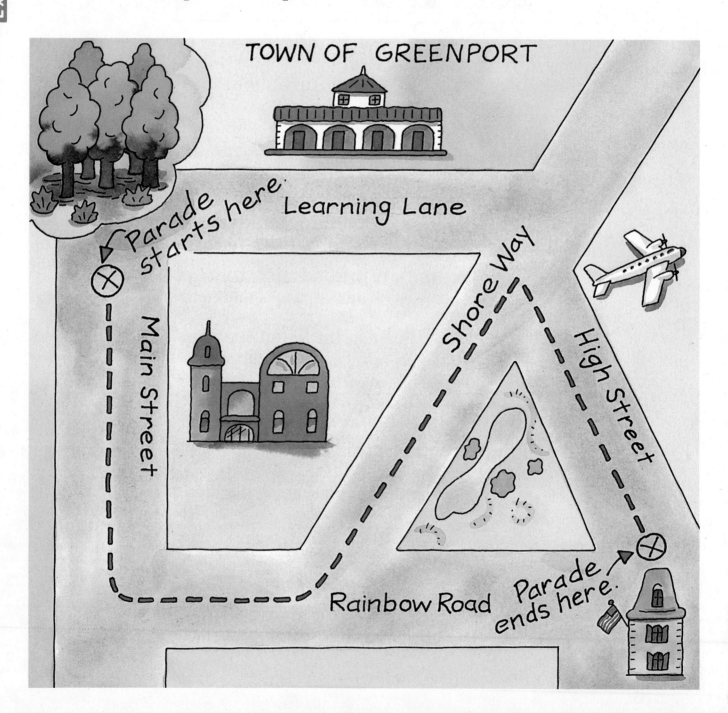

TOWN OF GREENPORT

Parade starts here

Learning Lane

Shore Way

Main Street

High Street

Rainbow Road

Parade ends here.

The map has pictures on it called **symbols**. The **key** tells you what each symbol means.

The symbol for Cape Airport looks like a plane. What is the symbol for Goose Lake?

The red line shows the parade route. A route is the path that someone or something takes.

Help Jody write about the parade. On another paper, list the streets and places the parade passed.

WRITING APPLICATION A Map

Imagine that you were in the parade with Jody. Write a narrative paragraph about it. Tell what you saw as you marched. Use street and place names from the map.

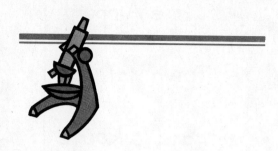

Writing About Science

You have written about doing things.
Scientists write about doing things, too.
Scientists study many parts of our world.
Then they write about what they have seen.

ACTIVITIES

Picture a Place

How would you like to be a scientist who
explores the world? Where would you go?
Draw a picture of yourself in a strange new
place. Share the picture with your class. Tell
where you are and what you see.

Write About Science

Look at the scientist on the next page.
Think about where she is and what she sees.
What do you think she will write in her journal?
Write a journal entry that you think
the scientist might write.

Respond to Literature

You do not have to travel far to be a scientist. *Science Fun with Mud and Dirt* by Rose Wyler tells about interesting experiments you can do with plain old dirt. Read this paragraph from the book. Then look at some dirt. Write a narrative paragraph about your experiment.

Science Fun with Mud and Dirt

Dirt can be almost any color—red, yellow, brown, black. It can even be pink or white. Yet all dirt is alike in one way. It is made of bits and pieces.

Look at some dirt with a magnifying glass and see the bits and pieces in it. Many kinds may be mixed together. Sort them out. Can you tell what they are?

UNIT CHECKUP

LESSON 1
Group Writing: A Narrative Paragraph
(page 92)   Circle the correct word.

The (indent, detail) sentences tell more about the main idea of a paragraph.

LESSON 2
Thinking: Stating the Main Idea (page 94)
Read the details. Then circle the main-idea sentence.

I looked for rocks. I watched a turtle.

 I went hiking.   ■ I found a snail.

LESSON 3
Writing a Paragraph (page 96) Write a paragraph telling about something that you might like to do if you lived a hundred years ago.

LESSON 4
Speaking and Listening (page 104)   Circle the name of the person you would introduce first if you wanted to introduce a grandfather and a little boy.

the grandfather   the little boy

LESSON 5
Maps (page 106)   Circle the correct word.

A (key, route) is a path someone takes.

You have thought about good times and fun things to do. Why not share what you have learned with others?

Look at this book. It lists fun things that children can do. Talk with your classmates about what might be in the book.

With your classmates, make a book about fun things to do.

- Brainstorm for activities to put in the book.
- Then write short paragraphs about how to do each activity. Put the steps in order.
- Draw pictures for each activity.
- Share the book with other classes in your school.

5

Verbs

JOURNAL

I am what I am! That's a great thing to be!
If I say so myself, HAPPY BIRTHDAY TO ME!

Dr. Seuss
from <u>Happy Birthday to You!</u>

1 WHAT IS A VERB?

A verb is a word that shows action.

Anna spins around.
Jake claps his hands.

Which words are verbs?

 Write each sentence. Then circle each verb.

Example: I wrap the gift.   I (wrap) the gift.

1. We play a funny game.

_____

- -

_____

2. Then, we sit at the table.

- -

_____

3. Mother brings the cake.

- -

_____

4. Dad lights the candles.

- -

_____

5. My friends sing a song.

_____

- -

_____

Extra Practice, page 135

![writing icon] **WRITING APPLICATION** A Sentence

Draw a picture of something you do at a birthday party.
Write a sentence that tells about it. Then, circle the verb
in your sentence.

You may wish to have the children orally identify the verb
in each sentence.

2 VERBS THAT TELL ABOUT THE PRESENT

Verbs can tell about actions that happen now. Time words like **now** and **today** tell you it is the present.

Add **s** to most verbs to tell what one person or thing does now.

Tim **wears** a hat now.
Mother and Ruth **blow** horns today.

Which verb tells what one person is doing now? How does the verb end?

 Tell which verb is correct.

Example: The children (laugh, laughs) today.
laugh

1. We (dance, dances) on New Year's Day.
2. Father (play, plays) his fiddle.
3. Grandmother (clap, claps) her hands.
4. Ruth and Tim (kick, kicks) up their feet.

REMEMBER

- Add **s** to most verbs to tell what one person or thing does now.

 Choose the correct verb. Then write each sentence.

Example: The phone (ring, rings) now.
The phone rings now.

5. Our friends (visit, visits) us today.

_____

- -

_____

6. Now, Jerry (open, opens) the door.

_____

- -

_____

7. Ben (shout, shouts) with joy.

_____

- -

_____

8. Fran and Grandma (hug, hugs).

_____

- -

_____

9. We (make, makes) a wish.

_____

- -

_____

Extra Practice, page 135

COOPERATIVE LEARNING

WRITING APPLICATION A Story

Work together. Imagine that today is New Year's Day.
Write a story about how you celebrate the day.
Circle the verbs in your story.

GRAMMAR: Verbs That Tell About the Present

Remind the children to look for clue words like *now* that indicate the present tense.

3 VERBS THAT TELL ABOUT THE PAST

Verbs can tell about actions that happened before now. Time words like **then** or **yesterday** tell you it is the past.

Add **ed** to most verbs to tell about actions in the past.

Yesterday, I **talked** about Martin Luther King Day.

How do you know that **talked** tells about the past?

 Tell how to make each verb in ( ) name an action that happened in the past.

Example: I (listen) to my teacher.   *listened*

1. Last week we (remember) Martin Luther King.
2. Yesterday, we (watch) a movie about him.
3. Dr. King (work) to help all people.
4. He (want) people to live in peace.

REMEMBER

- Add **ed** to most verbs to tell about actions in the past.

 Circle each verb that tells about the past. Then write the sentence.

Example: Yesterday, I (walk, (walked)) to the library.

Yesterday, I walked to the library.

5. I (open, opened) my book last night.

----

6. It (showed, shows) Martin Luther King.

----

7. He (talked, talks) to many people.

----

8. They (follows, followed) him.

----

9. They (wish, wished) for peace, too.

Extra Practice, page 135

WRITING APPLICATION A Story

With your classmates talk about a holiday named for a famous person. Then, write a story that tells what the person did.

GRAMMAR: Verbs That Tell About the Past

Point out that the *ed* ending is used with verbs that tell about one and more than one.

USING *BE*

The verb **be** has special forms to tell about the present and past.

Present	Past
I **am**	I **was**
He **is**	He **was**
We **are** You **are** They **are**	We **were** You **were** They **were**

 Tell which verb is correct.

Example: Today we (is, are) outside. *are*

1. I am glad it (is, are) Groundhog Day.
2. Last year we (was, were) in the woods.
3. The groundhog (was, were) asleep.
4. We hope it (is, are) awake today.

REMEMBER

- Use **am** with **I**. Use **is** to tell about one. Use **are** to tell about more than one.
- Use **was** for one. Use **were** for more than one.

Choose the correct verb. Then write each sentence.

Example: This holiday (am, is) exciting.
This holiday is exciting.

5. The groundhog (was, were) out yesterday.

- -

6. I (am, are) sure it saw a shadow.

- -

7. We (was, were) near the animal.

- -

8. The day (was, were) very cold.

- -

9. We (is, are) ready for more winter.

- -

Extra Practice, Practice Plus, pages 135–137

COOPERATIVE
LEARNING

WRITING APPLICATION A Story

Work with a partner. Imagine that you are groundhogs.
Write a story that tells what you do on Groundhog Day.
Circle all the forms of **be** in your story.

GRAMMAR: Using _be_   Have the children name the forms of _be_ that are singular and those that are plural.

5 USING *DO* AND *SEE*

The verbs **do** and **see** have special forms.

with	I, we, you, they	he, she, it
use	do │ see	does │ sees
	did │ saw	did │ saw

 Choose the correct verb. Then write each sentence.

Example: I (see, sees) my friends.
          I see my friends.

1. We (see, sees) all the hearts.

_____

- -

_____

2. I (does, did) not forget the holiday.

_____

- -

_____

3. Tony (see, sees) the card I made.

_____

- -

_____

4. Yesterday, Jan (see, saw) your card.

_____

- -

_____

Extra Practice, page 138

WRITING APPLICATION A Greeting Card

Make a Valentine's Day card. Use the verbs **do**
and **see** to write a few sentences inside the card about
the holiday.

6 USING *COME*, *GO*, AND *RUN*

The verbs **come**, **go**, and **run** are different from most verbs.

with	I, we, you, they	he, she, it
use	come | go | run	comes | goes | runs
	came | went | ran	came | went | ran

Choose the correct verb. Then write each sentence.

Example: A card (come, came) for Mother.
A card came for Mother.

1. Mother's Day (come, comes) in May.

- -

2. We (go, went) to the market yesterday.

- -

3. We (runs, ran) home to make breakfast.

- -

4. Now, Mother (come, comes) downstairs.

- -

Extra Practice, page 138

WRITING APPLICATION A Paragraph

Plan a Mother's Day celebration. Write a paragraph about the special day. Use the verbs **come**, **go**, and **run**. Circle each verb.

GRAMMAR: Using *come*, *go*, and *run*   You may wish to have the children orally identify the correct verbs.

7 USING *GIVE* AND *SING*

The verbs **give** and **sing** have special forms.

with	I, we, you, they	he, she, it
use	give | sing	gives | sings
	gave | sang	gave | sang

Choose the correct verb. Then write each sentence.

Example: Papa (sing, sings) on holidays.
Papa sings on holidays.

1. We (sings, sing) to Dad on Father's Day.

- -

2. Betty always (sing, sings) the loudest.

- -

3. Dad loves the song we (sings, sang).

- -

4. Now, we (gives, give) him a gift.

- -

Extra Practice, page 138

WRITING APPLICATION A Story

Write a story about a family that sings songs about holidays all day long. Use the verbs **sing** and **give** in your story.

GRAMMAR

USING *HAVE* AND *HAS*

The verb **have** is another special verb.

I or you	have
one person or thing	has
more than one person or thing	have

 Choose the correct verb. Then write each sentence.

Example: My friend (has, have) a camera.

My friend has a camera.

1. I (have, has) a horn.

- -

2. Jana (have, has) a hat to wear.

- -

3. The twins (have, has) little drums.

- -

4. Mother (have, has) lemonade for us.

- -

Extra Practice, page 138

![pencil icon] **WRITING APPLICATION** Sentences

Draw a picture of an Independence Day parade. Write a few sentences that tell about something each person has.

GRAMMAR: Using *have* and *has*   You may wish to have the children orally identify the correct verbs.

9 MECHANICS: Contractions

A **contraction** is a short form of two words.
An **apostrophe** ' takes the place of the letters
that are left out.

are not—aren't   have not—haven't
does not—doesn't   is not—isn't
do not—don't   cannot—can't
did not—didn't

Which letters does each apostrophe replace?

 Tell how to make the words in ( ) into a contraction. Then
read the new sentence.

Example: This (is not) a happy holiday. *isn't*

1. It (did not) stop raining all day.
2. We (cannot) go out on Columbus Day.
3. We (are not) having a parade.
4. I (do not) want to get wet.

REMEMBER

- A **contraction** is a short form of two words.
- An **apostrophe** takes the place of the letters that are left out.

 Write the contraction for the underlined words in each sentence.

Example: Please <u>do not</u> forget your gloves.

            don't

5. The Columbus Day parade <u>cannot</u> start. _____

6. They <u>are not</u> sure when it will begin. _____

7. The drummer <u>is not</u> here yet. _____

8. Marty <u>does not</u> have his gloves. _____

9. We <u>have not</u> worn our caps. _____

Extra Practice, page 139

WRITING APPLICATION A Diary Entry

Imagine that you are a sailor on Columbus's ship. Write a diary entry about your voyage.

MECHANICS: Contractions   Have the children write the words that make each contraction in their diary entries.

Name _____

10 VOCABULARY BUILDING: Time-order Words

Time-order words tell you what happens first and what happens next.

first   next   then   last   at last

First, we decide what we want to be.

Then, we make our costumes.

Last, we put them on.

 Tell the correct order of the sentences.

Example: First Last Next   *First Next Last*

1. First, we choose a big pumpkin.
2. Then, Mama cuts off the top.
3. Last, we make a scary face.
4. Next, we scoop out all the seeds.

VOCABULARY: Time-order Words   **127**

REMEMBER

■ **Time-order words** tell the order of events.

 Circle each time-order word. Then write the sentences in the correct order.

Example: (First,) I bought a mask.

Next, I go to school.

First, I wake up on Halloween.

At last, we have our costume parade.

Then, my teacher helps me put on my costume.

5. _____

_____

6. _____

_____

7. _____

_____

8. _____

Extra Practice, page 139

WRITING APPLICATION Vocabulary and Writing

Use time-order words to write a paragraph about how to make a mask.

VOCABULARY: Time-order Words   Remind the children to use the proper verb tenses when writing their paragraphs.

GRAMMAR AND WRITING CONNECTION

Combining Sentences

Parts of two sentences are sometimes the same. You can use **and** to make two sentences into one.

Roger came to the parade.
Fran came to the parade.

Roger **and** Fran came to the parade.

COOPERATIVE LEARNING

With your classmates tell which parts of each set of sentences are the same. Then tell how to combine each pair of sentences.

Example: We run.
We shout.
We run and shout.

1. A clown sang.
   A clown danced.

2. Jane marched.
   Kevin marched.

3. Dick clapped.
   Gina clapped.

4. A balloon floated.
   A balloon popped.

Marta wrote these sentences about Thanksgiving. Help Marta revise her sentences. Use **and** to combine the underlined words. Then write the new sentence.

Example: <u>Ken</u> dusted. <u>Jenny</u> dusted.
Ken and Jenny dusted.

5. Mom <u>roasted a turkey</u>. Mom <u>baked rolls</u>.

- -

6. Dad <u>made stuffing</u>. Dad <u>tossed the salad</u>.

- -

7. <u>Fran</u> set the table. <u>Roger</u> set the table.

- -

8. <u>Grandma</u> took pictures. <u>Grandpa</u> took pictures.

- -

9. Everyone <u>was hungry</u>. Everyone <u>ate too much</u>.

- -

Which is your favorite holiday? Write about it in a paragraph. Then see if you have repeated any words. Use **and** to combine sentences.

UNIT CHECKUP

LESSON 1

What Is a Verb? (page 114)   Read each sentence. Circle each verb.

1. My grandmother calls on my birthday.
2. She sings me a birthday song.
3. My friends send me a card.

LESSON 2

Verbs That Tell About the Present (page 115) Circle the correct verb.

4. We (visit, visits) Ed on New Year's Day.
5. He (make, makes) lunch for us.
6. Now, we (wear, wears) funny hats.

LESSON 3

Verbs That Tell About the Past (page 117) Circle each verb that tells about the past.

7. Dr. King (talk, talked) to many people.
8. He (marched, march) in our city.
9. He (dreamed, dreams) of peace.

LESSON 4

Using *be* (page 119)   Circle the correct verb.

10. The groundhog (was, were) out yesterday.
11. We (was, were) in the forest.
12. I (am, are) happy in the sunshine.

LESSON 5

Using *do* **and** *see* (page 121)   Circle the correct verb.

13. You (do, does) something special.
14. My friends (sees, see) your valentine.
15. Manuel (see, sees) my card.

UNIT CHECKUP

 LESSON 6

Using *come*, *go*, and *run* (page 122)   Circle the correct verb.

16. We (go, goes) out on Mother's Day.

17. Last year, we (go, went) to the beach.

 LESSON 7

Using *give* and *sing* (page 123)   Circle the correct verb.

18. I (sing, sings) on Father's Day.

19. I (give, gives) Dad a hug.

 LESSON 8

Using *have* and *has* (page 124)   Circle the correct verb.

20. We (have, has) a nice Independence Day.

21. John (have, has) a big red basket.

 LESSON 9

Mechanics: Contractions (page 125)   Circle the contraction for each numbered word.

22.   cannot   aren't   can't

23.   are not   aren't   isn't

24.   does not   don't   doesn't

 LESSON 10

Vocabulary Building: Time-order Words (page 127)
Write **1**, **2**, and **3** to put the sentences in the correct time order.

25. _____   Last, someone opens the door.

26. _____   First, you walk up to the door.

27. _____   Next, you knock.

CELEBRATE!

Play Happy Holidays with a partner. Choose a holiday from the first party bag. Tell your friend how you celebrated the day last year. Use some of the verbs from the second party bag. Take turns with your partner.

Halloween
Independence Day
Thanksgiving Day

play   sing
eat   come

give
decorate

HAPPY BIRTHDAY TO ME

Write a story about how you spent your last birthday. Use the words **first**, **then**, and **last** to tell when things happened.

Mask Parade

Use a large sheet of white paper to draw a mask. Use crayons and markers to decorate it. Then hold your mask up to your face and march around the room with your friends. Tell where you might wear your mask. Use the verbs **come** and **go**.

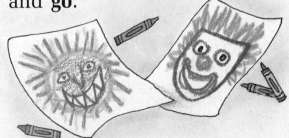

CREATIVE EXPRESSION

Often the words in a poem begin with the same letter or sound. This makes the poem fun to say and gives it a musical sound. Read this poem. Which sounds are repeated?

The Song of the Sour Plum

Ever eat a pickled plum?
A pink, puckered, pickled plum?
A spunky salty sprinkled plum?
Every inch a wrinkled plum?
A shrunken plum
A sting-y plum
Brr, brr, sour!

Translated by Ann Herring

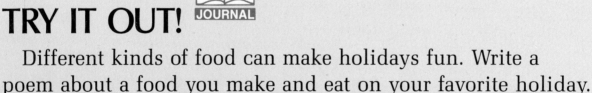

TRY IT OUT!

Different kinds of food can make holidays fun. Write a poem about a food you make and eat on your favorite holiday. Use words that sound alike. Try to use exact verbs to tell about the food.

EXTRA PRACTICE

What Is a Verb? (page 114) Circle each word that is a verb.

1. We plan a birthday party.
2. Mia wraps the gift.
3. Dad hangs balloons.

Verbs That Tell About the Present (page 115) Circle the correct verb.

4. Mario (sing, sings) on New Year's Day.
5. Today, Tina and Tad (laugh, laughs).
6. The children (hope, hopes) for snow.

Verbs That Tell About the Past (page 117) Circle the verb that tells about the past.

7. We (learn, learned) about Martin Luther King.
8. Then, Alva and I (asks, asked) questions.
9. Dr. King (work, worked) hard for peace.

Using *be* (page 119) Circle the correct verb.

10. Today (is, are) Groundhog Day.
11. We (was, were) in the woods this morning.
12. A groundhog (was, were) near a tree.

Additional practice for a difficult skill
Using *be* (page 119)

A. Read each sentence. Circle the form of **be** in each sentence.

13. Yesterday, my friend was in the forest.
14. Two groundhogs were by a rock.
15. Groundhogs are small animals.
16. Yesterday, I was in the library.
17. Terri was with me.
18. There were many books about animals.
19. This is a book about groundhogs.
20. I am glad I found this book.
21. Terri is happy, too.
22. We are good readers.

B. Write the correct form of **be** for each subject to complete the chart.

Subject	Present	Past
23. I		
24. You		
25. The child		
26. We		
27. The children		

C. Use a form of **be** to finish the story.

Now, it 28 time for our Groundhog party. Yesterday morning, we 29 baking. By noon, the kitchen 30 so hot! Then, last night, Jack 31 blowing up balloons. Now, I 32 excited. A winter party 33 fun for everyone. We 34 glad you can come today. Yesterday, you 35 not feeling well.

GRAMMAR

28. _____

29. _____

30. _____

31. _____

32. _____

33. _____

34. _____

35. _____

Using *do* and *see* (page 121)   Circle the correct verb.

36. You (do, does) not make a card.
37. Ana (do, did) not forget Valentine's Day.
38. She (see, saw) a pretty card yesterday.

Using *come*, *go*, and *run* (page 122)
Circle the correct verb.

39. Mother's Day (come, comes) once a year.
40. Yesterday, I (goes, went) to the store.
41. Kira (come, came) with me.

Using *give* and *sing* (page 123)   Circle the correct verb.

42. We (sing, sings) a Father's Day song.
43. Dad (sing, sings) with us.
44. I (give, gives) Dad a tie.

Using *have* and *has* (page 124)   Circle the correct verb.

45. We (has, have) an Independence Day show.
46. Lucy (has, have) a flag to wave.
47. I (has, have) a drum to beat.

Mechanics: Contractions (page 125) Write the contraction for the underlined words.

48. This Columbus Day <u>is not</u> sunny.

_____

- - - - - - - - - - - - - - - - - -

_____

49. I <u>do not</u> have an umbrella.

- - - - - - - - - - - - - - - - - -

_____

50. We <u>are not</u> going to the parade.

- - - - - - - - - - - - - - - - - -

_____

Vocabulary Building: Time-Order Words
(page 127) Write **1**, **2**, **3**, and **4** to put the sentences in the correct time order.

_____

- - - - - -

51. _____ Then, Anna goes to the Halloween party.

_____

- - - - - -

52. _____ First, Anna gets paper and paint.

_____

- - - - - -

53. _____ Last, Anna wins a prize.

_____

- - - - - -

54. _____ Next, she makes a mask.

GRAMMAR

MAINTENANCE

Unit 1: Sentences

Statements and Questions, Commands, and Exclamations (pages 3, 5, 7)   Read each sentence. Is it a **statement**, **question**, **command**, or **exclamation**? Write which kind of sentence it is.

1. Jerri moved to a large city.

   _____

2. Does she like her new home?

   _____

3. Look at Jerri smile.

   _____

4. How happy she is!

   _____

Parts of a Sentence (page 11)   Draw one line under the subject of each sentence. Draw two lines under the predicate.

5. Willie and Deb go to the airport.
6. Their parents carry a suitcase.
7. Many people wait by the airplane.

Beginning and Ending Sentences (page 13) Circle the end mark that completes each sentence.

8. Please tell me about our city hall   !   .
9. We will see it soon   .   ?
10. What an exciting day   !   .
11. How old is the building   .   ?

Unit 3: Nouns

Nouns for People, Places, and Things
(pages 61, 62)   Circle the noun in each sentence.
Write if it names a **person**, **place**, or **thing**.

12. My brother marches.   _____

13. Listen to that drum.   _____

14. There is the museum.   _____

Special Nouns (pages 63, 65)   Write each
sentence correctly.

15. There is a show on halloween.

_____

16. I hope jon brings his pony.

_____

17. I ride inky down fern road.

_____

More Than One (pages 67, 69)   Write each noun to name more than one.

18. horse _____

19. tooth _____

20. fox _____

21. branch _____

Titles and Dates (page 70)   Write each sentence correctly.

22. Our fair is on march 17 1990.

_____

_____

23. Last month ms. Ray sold tickets.

_____

_____

24. I bought one on february 9 1990.

_____

_____

Unit 5: Verbs

Verbs That Tell About the Present
Verbs That Tell About the Past (pages 115, 117)
Circle the correct verb.

25. Today, Al (plan, plans) a party.
26. Yesterday, I (paint, painted) a card.
27. Then, we (cleans, cleaned) the house.

Using *be*   Using *do* and *see* (pages 119, 121)
Circle the correct verb.

28. This Groundhog Day (is, are) sunny.
29. Now, we (see, saw) a groundhog.
30. Last year, it (does, did) not come out.

Using *come, go,* and *run* (page 122)   Circle
the correct verb.

31. Grandma (come, comes) on Mother's Day.
32. Last year, we (go, went) to her home.
33. Now, I (run, ran) to meet Grandma.
34. Then, Mom (come, came) upstairs.
35. Later, I (ran, runs) outside.

Using *give* and *sing*   Using *have* and *has*
(pages 123, 124)   Circle the correct verb.

36. Yesterday, Dad (gives, gave) me a hug.
37. Then, he (sing, sang) to Ned and me.
38. Today, I (have, has) a gift for Dad.
39. He (have, has) two gifts already.
40. Now, I (sing, sang) to Dad.

UNIT

6

Writing a Story

A good book is the best of friends. . . .

Martin Tupper

AWARD
WINNING
SELECTION

How do you make a birthday or happy day special? Read how Mole and Troll make a birthday special.

HAPPY BIRTHDAY, MOLE AND TROLL

by Tony Johnston

Notice how the author uses details to let you "see" the things that Mole makes for Troll's birthday.

One day Troll woke up excited. "Mole!" he shouted. "Come up!"
Mole came up. "What is it?" he asked.
"Do you know what day it is?" asked Troll.
"Tuesday," said Mole.

"I mean what **day** it is?" said Troll.

"Well, Troll, when you say it like that, I don't know."

"Are you sure?" asked Troll.

"I am sure."

"Guess what day it is, Mole. It is one of your favorite days."

"Christmas!" shouted Mole. "It is Christmas! Where is my present?"

"It is not Christmas. Guess again."

"Halloween. Boo!" cried Mole.

"It is not Halloween either," said Troll. "I will give you a hint."

"Good," said Mole. "A hint will help."

"It is somebody's birthday," said Troll.

That was a good hint. It was such a good hint, Mole knew whose birthday it was.

"Good-bye, Troll," he said quickly. "See you later." Mole hurried home.

He rustled in his desk. He found scissors, paper, doilies, ink, pencils, paste, and sequins. He went to work.

What does
Mole make?

Then he bustled in the kitchen. He found
flour, sugar, baking powder, eggs, milk,
vanilla, and chocolate. And he went to work.

In a little while, Mole called Troll.

"I am ready," he called.

"Ready for what?" asked Troll.

"For a surprise. Come and see."

Troll liked surprises. He came to see.

"Happy Birthday, Troll!" shouted Mole,
grinning from ear to ear.

Troll was really surprised. "Thank you,
Mole," he said. "Now I have a surprise for
you."

"What?"

"It is not **my** birthday."

Mole stared at Troll. "It isn't?"

"No," said Troll, patting him gently.

"Oh," groaned Mole. "How dumb of me."

"You are not dumb. You are kind. Who else would give me a party when it is not my birthday?"

"Troll?" asked Mole, "whose birthday is it?"

"That is the best surprise of all. It is **your** birthday!"

Mole sat down. "Well, isn't that nice," he muttered. "It is my birthday. It is MY BIRTHDAY!" he yelled.

Troll laughed. "Wait right here," he said.

"I will," said Mole. "I am too surprised to move."

Knock. Knock. Knock.

Mole opened the door. There was Troll with a big birthday cake.

"Happy Birthday, Mole!" he said, grinning from ear to ear.

"Oh, thank you, Troll!"

"You are welcome, Mole."

Then Mole said, "Wait right here."

He ran to the kitchen and came back with a big cake too.

"Happy Birthday, Troll!" he said.

"But it is **your** birthday," said Troll.

"I want to share it with you," said Mole.

Then they each made a wish and blew the candles out.

Thinking Like a Reader

1. What important day did Mole forget?
2. Have you ever forgotten an important day? What day was it?
3. What happened?

Write about it in your journal.

Thinking Like a Writer

4. How does the author let you know that Mole and Troll are good friends?
5. Suppose you were writing a story about a friend's birthday. What things would you tell your readers about the day?

Write your ideas in your journal.

Brainstorm *Vocabulary*

Mole and Troll speak politely to each other. What are some polite words that we should use? Make a Polite Word Chart in class. Include any new words in a personal word list.

Talk It Over *Tell a Chain Story*

Tell a chain story with your classmates about how Mole and Troll might celebrate a holiday. Sit in a circle with your classmates. Have one person start the story. Each person should add a part to the story as you go around the circle.

Quick Write *Add to a Story*

What do you think Mole and Troll did after they blew out the candles on the cake? Write a paragraph telling what they might have done.

Idea Corner *Think About Holidays*

In your journal, write some ideas for a holiday story. You might write topic ideas or draw pictures of favorite holidays.

Finding Ideas for Writing
Look at the pictures. Think about what you see.
What story ideas do the pictures give you?
Write your ideas in your journal.

A VALENTINE JUST FOR YOU

FOR YOU, VALENTINE

For Someone Very Special

1 GROUP WRITING: A Story

When you write a story, you want your readers to enjoy it. That is your **purpose** for writing. What does a story need?

- A Beginning, a Middle, and an End
- Ideas in Time Order

COOPERATIVE LEARNING

A Beginning, a Middle, and an End

Read the story. Notice the three parts.

Toby jumped out of bed. First, she looked at the calendar. Toby saw it was Valentine's Day.

Next, she went out with a shovel.

Last, Toby dug a heart in the snow.

The **beginning** of a story tells what the story is about. The **middle** tells what happens. The **end** tells how it turns out.

Guided Practice: A Beginning, a Middle, and an End

Work with your class to label each story part as the beginning, middle, or end.

1. She planted it in the ground.
2. Maria took the little tree outside.
3. On Arbor Day Papa gave Maria a tiny tree.

Putting Ideas in Time Order

Look at the story about Toby again. The sentences are in time order. When you write a story, use time-order words like **first**, **next**, and **last** to tell the order of events.

Putting a Story Together

A chart can help you write the beginning, middle, and end of a story.

Here is Lee's chart.

Beginning	Middle	End
Sid put on his Halloween mask.	Sid went to a Halloween parade.	Sid won a prize for his mask.

Guided Practice: Writing a Story

Choose a holiday for a story. Make a chart. Write a beginning, a middle, and an end.

Checklist: A Story

Complete this checklist. You may use it when you write a story.

CHECKLIST

✔ Purpose and audience
✔ A beginning, a middle, and an end

✔ Ideas in _____

    First
    Next

    _____

2 THINKING AND WRITING: Predicting Outcomes

A good story keeps you guessing about how it will end. As you read, look for clues. Then guess what will happen next.

A writer must make sure the story ending fits the clues. If the ending does not fit, the readers will be confused.

Read Gary's notes for a story.

> Holly wants to buy a gift for Dad. She knows he likes tools. Holly looks in the garage to see what Dad needs. Then she goes to the store. She looks at a hammer, a tie, and a book. She decides what to buy for Dad.

Thinking Like a Writer

■ What will Holly buy? Why?

Gary will have Holly buy the hammer because Dad likes tools. When you write a story, make sure your ending fits all the clues.

Read each writer's notes. Circle the ending that fits all of the clues.

1. Brian wants to be in the Columbus Day play. He has one week to get ready.
   - ■ Brian eats pizza all week.
   - ■ Brian makes a costume.

2. Betsy wanted to remember Flag Day. She decided to make a poster.
   - ■ Betsy bought paper and paints.
   - ■ Betsy bought a needle and thread.

3. Dan plans a surprise for Mother's Day. He knows Mom loves flowers.
   - ■ Dan plants roses.
   - ■ Dan plants beans.

3 INDEPENDENT WRITING: A Story

Prewrite: Step 1

A story must have a beginning, a middle, and an end.

Here is how Todd chose a story topic.

Choosing a Topic

First, Todd wrote a list of holidays.
Next, he thought about each holiday.
Last, he chose the holiday to write about.

> Mother's Day
>
> Independence Day
>
> Thanksgiving

Todd decided to write about Thanksgiving. He explored his topic by making a Question Chart. A Question Chart answers questions that ask *who*, *when*, *where*, *what*, and *how*.

Exploring Ideas: Charting Strategy

> Who   a girl
> Where   a big city
> When   Thanksgiving Day
> What   The girl goes to a parade. She grabs a balloon and flies away.
> How   She lands when the wind stops.

Todd thought about his **audience** and **purpose** for writing. He looked at his chart. Then he made some changes.

Who   a girl Ana
Where   a big city Grandview
When   Thanksgiving Day
What   The girl goes to a parade. She grabs a balloon and flies away.
How   She lands when the wind stops.

Thinking Like a Writer

- How did Todd change his plan? Why?

YOUR TURN

JOURNAL

Think of a holiday story you would like to write. Use **Pictures** or your journal for ideas. Follow these steps.

- Make a list of holidays.
- Choose one you like best.
- Make a question chart.
- Change your chart if necessary.
- Think about your purpose and audience.

Write a First Draft: Step 2

Todd made a checklist to help him write a first draft. Here is Todd's first draft.

> Last thanksgiving Ana go to a nice parade. Clowns dance. Clowns sang. I like clowns.
>
> Ana grabbed a balloon Next, the wind blew and Ana flew away.
>
> She sailed in a window.

Planning Checklist
- Remember purpose and audience.
- Include a beginning, a middle, and an end.
- Put the sentences in time order.
- Use time-order words.

YOUR TURN

Write your first draft for a holiday story. Ask yourself these questions.

- What will my audience want to know?
- How can I use time order well?

TIME-OUT You might want to take some time out before you revise. Think about what you want to change.

Revise: Step 3

After he finished his first draft, Todd read it over to himself. Then, he shared his writing with a classmate. He wanted ideas for making his story better.

Todd looked back at his planning checklist to make sure his story was complete. He put a check next to the step he forgot. He now has a checklist to use as he revises.

Todd revised his story. He did not correct small mistakes. He knew he could fix them later, after he had made the more important changes.

Revising Checklist
- Remember purpose and audience.
- Include a beginning, a middle, and an end.
- Put the sentences in time order.
- ✔ Use time-order words.

Here is Todd's revised story.

> Last thanksgiving Ana go to a nice ~~great~~
> parade. Clowns dance. Clowns ~~and~~
> sang. I like clowns.
>   Then, Ana grabbed a balloon Next, the
> wind blew and Ana flew away.
>   At last She sailed in a window. There
> was Grandma!

WISE WORD CHOICE

Thinking Like a Writer

- What time-order words did Todd add?
- Do you think Todd's changes made the story better? Why?

YOUR TURN

Read your story. Ask yourself these questions. Then revise your story.

- Does my beginning make readers want to keep reading?
- Do I tell enough in the middle of my story?
- Does my ending fit the beginning and the middle? Do I like my ending?

Proofread: Step 4

Todd knew that his story would not be complete until he proofread it. He used this proofreading checklist.

Here is part of Todd's proofread story.

> went great
> Last thanksgiving Ana go to a nice
> danced and
> parade. Clowns dance. Clowns
>
> sang. I like clowns.
> Then,
> ∧Ana grabbed a balloon. Next, the

YOUR TURN

Proofreading Practice

Proofread this paragraph. Use proofreading marks to correct the mistakes.

> Yesterday is father's Day. Andy did not have enough money to buy his father a gift? That afternoon he paint a picture for his father.

Proofreading Checklist
- Did I indent each paragraph?
- Did I use capital letters correctly?
- Did I use the correct end marks?

Applying Your Proofreading Skills

Now proofread your story. Read your checklist again. Review **The Grammar Connection** and **The Mechanics Connection**, too. Use proofreading marks to correct mistakes.

Proofreading Marks

∧   Add
—   Take out
≡   Make a capital letter
/   Make a small letter

THE GRAMMAR CONNECTION

Remember these rules about verbs.

■ Add **s** to most verbs to tell what one person or thing does in the present.

    Beth clap**s**. We clap.

■ Add **ed** to most verbs to tell about actions in the past.

    Yesterday, the band march**ed**.

THE MECHANICS CONNECTION

Remember these rules about contractions and apostrophes.

■ A **contraction** is a short form of two words.

■ An **apostrophe** takes the place of the letters that are left out.

    do not = **don't**

Publish: Step 5

Todd wanted to share his story with his friends. He used his best handwriting to copy his story. Then he drew a picture to go with his story. He held up the picture as he read the story to his friends.

YOUR TURN

Make a final copy of your story for your classmates. Use your best handwriting. Here are some other ways to share your story.

SHARING SUGGESTIONS

Make masks for your story characters. Use the masks to put on a play.	Draw pictures for each part of your story. Have a friend put the pictures in order while you read the story.	Read your story to classmates. Have them try to guess the ending. Then read your ending to them.

4 SPEAKING AND LISTENING: Telling a Story

You can use what you know about writing a story to tell a story to others.

First, write a few sentences about the beginning, the middle, and the end of your story on a note card.

NOTES — Independence Day at Camp

Beginning — It was Independence Day at Camp Daisy.

Middle — The children put on a show.

End — After the show they had a party.

Use these guidelines for telling your story.

SPEAKING GUIDELINES: Telling a Story

1. Think about the beginning, the middle, and the end of your story.
2. Make a note card to practice your talk.
3. Use time-order words.
4. Speak loudly and clearly.

- Why is it important to include a beginning, a middle, and an end to my story?
- How do time-order words help my listeners?

SPEAKING APPLICATION Telling a Story

Think of the holiday story that you wrote. Make a note card to help you tell the story. Use the speaking guidelines.

Use these guidelines as you listen to others tell their stories.

LISTENING GUIDELINES: Telling a Story

1. Look at the speaker.
2. Listen for the beginning, the middle, and the end.
3. Listen for time-order words to help you follow the story.

5 WRITER'S RESOURCES: ABC Order of Words

The alphabet is in **ABC order**. You can put words in ABC order, too.

age	These words are in ABC order.
birthday	Each word begins with a different
card	letter. The **first** letter of each word is used to put the words in order.
happy	These words are in ABC order.
heart	Each word begins with the same letter.
holiday	The **second** letter of each word is used to put them in order.

 Write each set of words in ABC order.

1. surprise   gift   open

2. turkey   time   today

3. parade   proud   people

WRITING APPLICATION ABC Order of Words

Make a list of words that tell about a holiday. Write the words in ABC order.

WRITER'S RESOURCES:
The Dictionary

The words in a **dictionary** are in ABC order. A dictionary is a book that tells what words mean. The words the dictionary tells about are called **entry words**.

---

school/store

school A place for teaching and learning.
speak To say or talk.
store A place for buying and selling things.

Each dictionary page has two guide words at the top. The **guide word** on the **left** tells the first word on the page. The guide word on the **right** tells the last word on the page.

 Use the dictionary page above to answer each question.

1. What is the meaning of *school*?

2. Which word comes after the word *speak*?

3. Name the guide words on the page.

WRITING APPLICATION The Dictionary

Use the dictionary in this book to write the guide words and meanings for each word.
holiday   month   birthday   invitation

Writing About Music

Musicians write songs about many different things. They often write songs about holidays or happy times.

ACTIVITIES

Picture a Song

Talk about holiday songs with your classmates. Pick one that tells a story. Draw a picture of the beginning, middle, and end of that song.

Write About a Song

Now write a story about the song you chose. Tell about the people, places, and things in the song.

Respond to Literature

Not all special days are holidays. Sometimes just being with someone special makes a day happy. *Georgia Music* by Helen V. Griffith tells how a grandfather and his granddaughter share special days.

Read this part of the book. Then think about a time you shared music with someone else. It might have been a holiday or just a happy day. Write a story about that time.

Georgia Music

In the evenings the two of them sat out on the rickety porch steps and the old man played tunes on his mouth organ. He knew a lot of songs and he taught the words to the girl so she could sing with the music.

The old man said he was really playing for the crickets and the grasshoppers because they made music for him in the daytime. He said they liked it, and the girl thought so, too.

UNIT CHECKUP

LESSON 1

Group Writing: A Story (page 154)   Write the story in the correct order.

Then, Molly sewed a cape.

First, Molly made a paper crown.

Last, she painted a mask.

LESSON 2

Thinking: Predicting Outcomes (page 156)   Write an ending for this story that makes sense.

Tomorrow is Valentine's Day. Dara buys red paper and lace. Then she runs home.

LESSON 3

Writing a Story (page 158)   Read this story beginning. Write the ending.

Mr. Goat was happy it was April Fools' Day. He planned to play tricks on people.

LESSON 4

Speaking and Listening (page 166)   Write the three parts of a story that you should include when you tell a story to others.

5

The Dictionary (page 169)   Circle the word that completes this sentence.

The guide word on the left tells the (first, last) word on a dictionary page.

THEME PROJECT CREATE A HOLIDAY

You have been thinking about holidays you know. Now think about making up your own holiday.

Talk with your classmates about what holiday you might celebrate. Brainstorm a list of ideas to share.

Write about a new holiday.
- Tell when and how it is celebrated.
- Note what special foods, if any, are eaten.
- Make a greeting card for your holiday.
- Tell your classmates about the holiday.

UNIT

7

Adjectives

If I could have
Any wish that could be
I wish that a dog
Could have me.

Eve Merriam

175

1 WHAT IS AN ADJECTIVE?

An adjective is a word that describes a noun.

Alissa found an old well.

Which word describes the noun **well**?

 Write each sentence. Then circle the adjective.

Example: I sit in the green grass.

I sit in the (green) grass.

1. Jay looked at the big well.

- -

2. Nan touched the rough bricks.

- -

3. She threw in a bright coin.

- -

4. They heard a soft splash.

- -

5. They made a secret wish.

- -

Extra Practice, page 193

 **WRITING APPLICATION** Sentences

Imagine that you have a wishing well. Write three sentences that describe the well. Then, underline the adjective in each sentence.

GRAMMAR: Adjectives   Have the children orally identify the adjective in each sentence.

2 ADJECTIVES THAT TELL HOW MANY

Some adjectives tell how many.

There were many candles on the cake.
Carl made three wishes.

Which adjectives tell how many?

 Write each sentence. Then circle the adjective that tells how many.

Example: I saw many friends.   *I saw* (many) *friends.*

1. I had eight candles.

----

2. I blew out every candle.

----

3. I made one wish.

----

4. Two children clapped.

----

5. We played some games.

Extra Practice, page 193

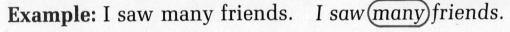 **WRITING APPLICATION** A Plan

Use adjectives that tell how many to write a plan for a class party.

3 USING *A* AND *AN*

The words **a** and **an** are special adjectives.

Use **a** before a word that begins with a consonant sound.

I always wanted **a** cow.

Use **an** before a word that begins with a vowel sound.

I would like **an** ox, too.

Which word comes before each noun?
How does each noun begin?

 Write **a** or **an** to complete each sentence.

Example: Do you have ___ pet?   *a*

1. I have always wanted _____ animal.

2. Once I wished for _____ octopus.

3. Then, I wanted _____ rabbit.

4. Next, I dreamed of _____ owl.

5. Now, I want _____ puppy.

Extra Practice, page 193

COOPERATIVE
LEARNING

WRITING APPLICATION A List

Make a list of animals. Exchange lists with a classmate.
Write the adjective **a** or **an** in front of the name of the
animals on each other's lists.

4 ADJECTIVES THAT COMPARE

You can use adjectives to compare.
You can add **er** to some adjectives to compare two nouns.

The pool is **deeper** than the pond.

You can add **est** to an adjective to compare more than two nouns.

It is the **deepest** pool of all.

Which adjective compares two nouns?
Which adjective compares more than two nouns?

 Tell whether to add **er** or **est** to each adjective.

Example: The pool is the new in the state.
   newest

1. The pool is warm than the sea.
2. The water is the clean in town.
3. This lane is wide than that one.
4. The diving board is the high of all.

REMEMBER

- Add **er** or **est** to an adjective to compare nouns.

 Add **er** or **est** to the adjective in ( ) in each sentence. Then write the new word.

Example: Miss Fay is the (kind) swimming teacher of all.

   kindest

5. I am a (fast) swimmer than Ed is.

---

6. He is (old) than I am.

---

7. He has the (smooth) stroke on the team.

---

8. Kim is the (young) girl on the team.

---

9. I wish I could be (strong) than she is.

Extra Practice, Practice Plus, pages 193–196

 **WRITING APPLICATION** A Story

Imagine that you are watching a swimming race. Write a story about the race. Use adjectives that compare to talk about the swimmers.

GRAMMAR: Adjectives That Compare   Have children tell the number compared in each sentence.

5 SYNONYMS AND ANTONYMS

A **synonym** is a word that has the same or almost the same meaning as another word.

> Martin wants to be a **great** author.
> Martin wants to be a **fine** author.

Antonyms are words with opposite meanings.

> He will write **sad** stories.
> He will write **happy** stories.

Name another synonym for **great**.
Name another antonym for **sad**.

 Read each pair of words. Tell if the words are synonyms or antonyms.

Example: laugh   cry   *antonyms*

1. warm   hot
2. hate   love
3. evening   day
4. begin   start
5. thick   thin

REMEMBER

- A **synonym** is a word that has the same or almost the same meaning as another word.
- **Antonyms** are words with opposite meanings.

Write a synonym or an antonym for the underlined word in each sentence.
Use the words in the box below.

Example: old tall

Ana sits under a <u>short</u> tree. *tall*

wild	outside	large	tidy

6. Ana wants to work in a <u>big</u> park.

- -

7. She likes to be <u>inside</u> all day.

- -

8. She will care for <u>tame</u> animals.

- -

9. Ana can keep the trails <u>clean</u>.

- -

Extra Practice, page 197

**COOPERATIVE
LEARNING**

WRITING APPLICATION A Paragraph

Write a paragraph about a job you would like. Exchange your paper with a partner. Write synonyms and antonyms for three of the adjectives in the paragraph.

GRAMMAR: Synonyms and Antonyms   Have the children orally identify their answers as synonyms or antonyms.

6 MECHANICS: Using Commas with Names of Places

You have learned to use capital letters when you write the names of places. Use a comma between the name of a city and a state when you write the two place names together.

Juan went to Denver, Colorado.

 Tell where the comma belongs in each sentence.

Example: Jed lives in Reno Nevada.
Reno, Nevada

1. Jed wants to fly to Austin Texas.
2. Then, he will visit Portland Oregon.
3. Next, he will go to Bangor Maine.
4. He might see Fulton Missouri.
5. Finally, he will stop at Provo Utah.

REMEMBER

- A **comma** is used between the names of a city and a state.

 Write the city and the state named in each sentence. Then, put the comma in the correct place.

Example: Would you like to visit Logan Utah?
Logan, Utah

6. Betty and Jim live in Albany New York.

- -

7. Betty wished to visit Rexburg Idaho.

- -

8. Jim wanted to see Dover Ohio.

- -

9. They thought about Salina Kansas.

- -

10. A friend suggested Orlando Florida.

- -

Extra Practice, page 197

WRITING APPLICATION A Paragraph

Write a paragraph about two cities you want to visit. Use adjectives to describe each place. Use commas when you write the name of a city and a state together.

MECHANICS: Using Commas with Places

Remind the children to capitalize correctly.

7 VOCABULARY BUILDING: Prefixes

A **prefix** is a word part added to the beginning
of a word.

Prefix	Meaning	Example
un	not, the opposite of	un + lock = **un**lock
re	again, back	re + fill = **re**fill

What does **un** mean?

What does **re** mean?

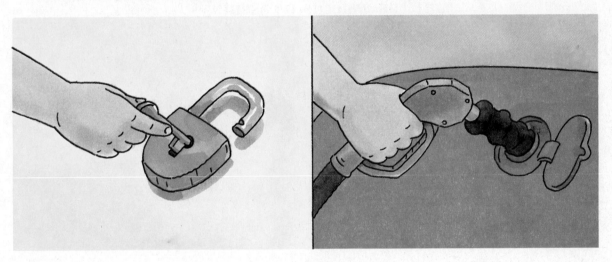

 Tell which words below have prefixes.
Then use the meaning of each prefix to tell what the word
means.

Example: Yesterday Cy was unwell.
    unwell   not well

1. Cy felt unhappy.
2. He wished he could rebuild his boat.
3. His brother was unable to help.
4. He reread the instructions.
5. Then he uncovered the tool box.

REMEMBER

- A **prefix** is a word part added to the beginning of a word.
- The prefix **un** means "not," or "the opposite of."
- The prefix **re** means "again," or "back."

 Add the prefix in ( ) to the underlined word in each sentence. Then write the sentence.

Example: (re) Dad <u>fills</u> the tank.
Dad refills the tank.

6. (re) Ali <u>folds</u> her towel.

- -

7. (un) The water is <u>pleasant</u>.

- -

8. (re) Dad <u>ties</u> the boat.

- -

9. (un) He is <u>sure</u> of the weather.

- -

10. (re) He <u>zips</u> his jacket.

- -

Extra Practice, page 197

WRITING APPLICATION Vocabulary and Writing

Imagine that you have a boat that can sail anywhere you wish. Write about a trip you make across the sea. Circle any words with the prefix **un** or **re**.

VOCABULARY: Prefixes   Have the children compile a class list of words with the prefix **un** or **re**.

GRAMMAR AND WRITING CONNECTION

Using Adjectives in Sentences

Use exact adjectives to make your sentences clear and interesting.

> I hope you get a *nice* cat.
> I hope you get a *gray* cat.

Which sentence tells you more about the cat? Why?

COOPERATIVE LEARNING

With your classmates look at the chart below. The adjectives at the top do not tell much about the picture. Write more exact adjectives in the chart.

	nice	good
cat		
woman		
park		

Change the underlined adjective in each sentence to a more exact adjective. Use the words from the box, or think of your own words. Rewrite each sentence.

Example: Vic is a <u>nice</u> boy.   *Vic is a kind boy.*

special	kind	colorful
four	happy	wonderful
sunny	helpful	clean

1. Vic made <u>nice</u> wishes.

----

2. He wanted people to feel <u>nice</u>.

----

3. He wished for <u>nice</u> weather.

----

4. Vic hoped for <u>nice</u> flowers.

----

5. He wished for a <u>nice</u> city.

Read this story starter. Then finish the story.
Use exact adjectives.

One night Patti made a special wish for all the children at her school.

GRAMMAR AND WRITING CONNECTION: Using Adjectives in Sentences

Name _____

UNIT CHECKUP

What Is an Adjective? (page 176)   Read each sentence. Then circle the adjective.

1. Kim found a yellow well.
2. She tossed a new coin.
3. She made a special wish.

Adjectives That Tell How Many (page 177)   Read each sentence. Then circle the adjective that tells how many.

4. Kira invited many friends to her party.
5. They sang several songs.
6. Soon Kira's mother lit seven candles.

Using *a* and *an* (page 178)   Write **a** or **an** to complete each sentence. _____

7. Karen and Carlos wanted _____ pet.

8. Karen wanted _____ alligator.

9. Carlos wished he could have _____ dog.

Adjectives That Compare (page 179)   Add **er** or **est** to the adjective in ( ) in each sentence. Write the new word. _____

10. Tina wants to be (strong) than Ali is. _____

11. Jan is the (strong) girl in the class. _____

12. She is (short) than Sandy is. _____

UNIT CHECKUP

LESSON 5

Synonyms and Antonyms (page 181)   Write the synonym or antonym for the underlined word in each sentence. Use the words from the word box.

big   wonderful   many

13. Jill wants to be a <u>good</u> doctor. _____

14. She will help <u>few</u> people. _____

15. Jill will work in a <u>huge</u> hospital. _____

LESSON 6

Mechanics: Using Commas with Places (page 183)
Put a comma in the correct place.

16. Len wished to see Miami Florida.

17. Gus went to Groves Texas.

18. The men went to Gary Indiana.

LESSON 7

Vocabulary Building: Prefixes (page 185)   Add the prefix in ( ) to the underlined word in each sentence. Then write the new word.

19. (un) I <u>tie</u> my shoe laces. _____

20. (re) Dad <u>fills</u> my air tank. _____

21. (re) I <u>read</u> the safety rules. _____

WISHBONES

Many foods are fun to eat. Foods can be fun to talk about, too.
Use adjectives when you talk about foods. For example,
a peach is red and yellow, round, fuzzy, soft, and sweet.
Take turns playing this game with a partner. Choose a food
from the wishbone, but do not tell your partner what it is.
Use adjectives to describe the food.
Then have your partner
guess the food.

orange   cherry
spaghetti   carrot
raisin   popcorn

FLIP FLOP

Play a game of opposites by using adjectives that compare two
things or more than two things. Read each sentence.
Write the opposite of the word in ( ). Add **er** or **est**.

Example: Beth is (short) than I am.

   taller

1. I wish I had a (big) bed than Jan has.

2. Beth has a (hard) pillow than Tina has.

3. Ana's slippers are the (old) ones here.

SUMMER SENSES

Do you wish it were summer?
You can imagine that it is.
Read each word on the beach
blanket. On each line write an
adjective for each word. Then,
on a separate sheet of paper,
draw a picture about summer.

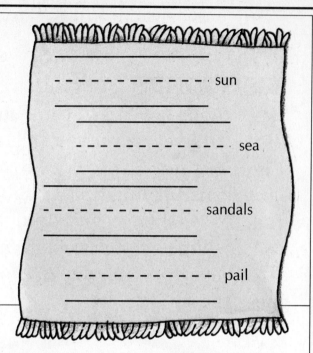

sun

sea

sandals

pail

ABC ADJECTIVES

Have a word race with your friends. Write six adjectives on a
sheet of paper. Then trade papers with one of your friends. See
who can be the first to write the words again, but in ABC order.

WEATHER WATCH

Did you need a hat yesterday? Did you wear your gloves? Make
a calendar for one week. Each day write two adjectives that tell
about the weather for the day. Finish your calendar with a
picture for each day.

Sun.	Mon.	Tue.	Wed.	Thu.	Fri.	Sat.

EXTRA PRACTICE

What Is an Adjective? (page 176)   Circle the adjective in each sentence.

1. Our well is on a steep hill.
2. We throw in shiny pennies.
3. The icy water splashes us.

Adjectives That Tell How Many (page 177)   Circle each word that tells how many.

4. My sister is two years old.
5. I put some candles on her cake.
6. One candle is for good luck.

Using *a* and *an* (page 178)   Read each sentence. Circle the correct word in (   ).

7. Every day I make (a, an) wish.
8. I wish for (a, an) animal.
9. I want (a, an) horse.

Adjectives That Compare (page 179)   Circle **er** or **est** to complete each underlined word.

10. Sumi is the <u>tall</u> girl in the gym class.
    (er, est)
11. Yoko wishes she were <u>strong</u> than I am.
    (er, est)
12. Juan is a <u>fast</u> runner than Al. (er, est)

Additional practice for a difficult skill
Adjectives That Compare
(page 179)

A. Write the correct **er** and **est** form of each adjective.

13. hard

_____   _____

- - - - - - - - - - - - - -   - - - - - - - - - - - - - -

_____   _____

14. sweet

_____   _____

- - - - - - - - - - - - - -   - - - - - - - - - - - - - -

_____   _____

15. bright

_____   _____

- - - - - - - - - - - - - -   - - - - - - - - - - - - - -

_____   _____

16. warm

_____   _____

- - - - - - - - - - - - - -   - - - - - - - - - - - - - -

_____   _____

17. loud

_____   _____

- - - - - - - - - - - - - -   - - - - - - - - - - - - - -

_____   _____

Name _____

B. Write the correct form of the underlined adjective to complete each sentence.

18. I have <u>old</u> sneakers.

Mike has _____ sneakers than I have.

Tad has the _____ sneakers of all.

19. Jane's baseball glove is <u>new</u>.

Mary's glove is _____ than Jane's glove.

Linda's glove is the _____ of all.

20. The pool is <u>cold</u>.

The lake is _____ than the pool.

The sea is the _____ of them all.

21. I am a <u>fast</u> runner.

You are a _____ runner than I am.

Ana is the _____ runner of us all.

22. My baseball cap is <u>tight</u>.

Tad's cap is _____ than mine is.

Al's cap is the _____ one of all.

PRACTICE PLUS: Lesson 4   195

C. Write the correct form of the underlined adjective to complete the second sentence.

Example: John and Jack are <u>tall</u> boys.

John is the ___ boy.

John is the taller boy.

23. Cory and Sal are <u>young</u> runners.

_____

- - - - - - - - - - - - - -

Cory is the _____ runner.

24. I see three <u>strong</u> swimmers.

_____

- - - - - - - - - - - - - -

Vera is the _____ swimmer.

25. Our school has a <u>deep</u> pool.

_____

- - - - - - - - - - - - - -

Your school has a _____ pool.

26. Three <u>small</u> girls climb the ropes.

_____

- - - - - - - - - - - - - -

Ella is the _____ climber.

27. Those two ropes are <u>long</u>.

_____

- - - - - - - - - - - - - -

That rope is _____ than this one.

28. Terri and Joe are <u>fast</u> climbers.

_____

- - - - - - - - - - - - - -

Terri is the _____ climber.

29. I see three <u>soft</u> mitts.

_____

- - - - - - - - - - - - - -

The black mitt is the _____ one of all.

Synonyms and Antonyms (page 181)

Read each pair of words. Circle **synonym** if the words are synonyms. Circle **antonym** if the words are antonyms.

30. fast   quick   synonym   antonym
31. little   small   synonym   antonym
32. clean   dirty   synonym   antonym

Mechanics: Using Commas with Places

(page 183)   Put a comma in the correct place in each sentence.

33. I want to see Los Angeles California.
34. Suzy wants to visit Detroit Michigan.
35. Pedro dreams of Tampa Florida.

Vocabulary Building: Prefixes (page 185)

Add the prefix in ( ) to the underlined word in each sentence. Then write the sentence.

36. (re) I <u>ran</u> our home movie.

----

37. (un) See how I <u>tie</u> the boat.

----

38. (re) Ed helps me <u>place</u> the oars.

GRAMMAR

UNIT

8

Writing a Description

Keep a poem in your pocket
and a picture in your head.

Beatrice Schenk de Regniers

Everyone likes the magic of wishes. These poems tell about different kinds of wishes. What do you wish for?

A Wish Is Quite a Tiny Thing

A wish is quite a tiny thing
    Just like a bird upon the wing,
It flies away all fancy free
And lights upon a house or tree;
It flies across the farthest air,
And builds a safe nest anywhere.

—Annette Wynne

Song For a Hot Day

Do you know what I could wish?
Five ripe cherries on a dish,
cherries very red and bright
on a dish that's very white
every cherry with its stem
and a fine dish under them—
oh, how sweet, how sweet, how sweet!
First I'd look and then I'd eat!

—Elizabeth Coatsworth

The Animal Store

If I had a hundred dollars to spend,
    Or maybe a little more,

I'd hurry as fast as my legs would go
    Straight to the animal store.

I wouldn't say, "How much for this or that?"
    "What kind of dog is he?"

I'd buy as many as rolled an eye,
    Or wagged a tail at me!

I'd take the hound with the drooping ears
    That sits by himself alone;

Cockers and Cairns and wobbly pups
    For to be my very own.

I might buy a parrot all red and green,
And the monkey I saw before,
If I had a hundred dollars to spend,
Or maybe a little more.

—Rachel Field

Whistle Wish

I wish that I could whistle
    Like my sister Wilma Rae,
What fun to pucker up and
    Puff out pleasing sounds all day.

I'd whistle in the morning
    As I rode the bus to school,
And even whistle—GLUB GLUB—
    In our local swimming pool.

Oh, what a noisy, happy place
    This world would surely be,
If Wilma Rae would pass
    Some whistle wisdom down to me.

—Constance Andrea Keremes

Thinking Like a Reader
1. Think about the poems you read. How are they alike? How are they different?
2. Which poem did you like the best? Why?

Write your thoughts in your journal.

Thinking Like a Writer
3. Look at the poem by Annette Wynne. Do you agree that a wish is "quite a tiny thing"?
4. How would you describe a wish if you were writing a poem?

Write your answers in your journal.

Brainstorm *Vocabulary*

All the poems you read use rhyming words. Write these words in your journal. Add two more rhyming words to each set. Include any new words in a personal word list.

thing, wing	bright, white	school, pool

Talk It Over *Recite a Poem of Your Own*

Make up a poem describing a food that you like. Then, say your poem out loud in class. Ask your classmates what they "saw" in their minds when they heard your poem.

Quick Write *Write an Ad*

Think about a pet you wish you could have. Then write a Want Ad describing the pet. Here is a Want Ad for a pet cat.

> **WANT AD** I would like a pet cat. It should have long whiskers and white fur.

Idea Corner *Think About Wishes*

You have read poems about wishes. What wish would you write about in a paragraph? Write your ideas in your journal.

Finding Ideas for Writing
Look at the pictures. Think about what you see.
What ideas do the pictures give you for descriptive writing?
Write your ideas in your journal.

GROUP WRITING: A Description

The **purpose** of description is to give a clear picture of a person, place, or thing. What makes a description clear to your **audience**?

- Main idea
- Descriptive details
- Grouping details

Main Idea
Descriptive Details

A main-idea sentence tells what a paragraph is about. Detail sentences tell more about the main idea. Descriptive details tell how things look, sound, taste, feel, or smell.

> The street fair was wonderful. Hot buns smelled fresh and tasted sweet. There were smooth red apples for sale.

Guided Practice:
Using Descriptive Details

As a class, choose a favorite food. Think of descriptive words to describe it. Work together to make a chart like this one.

Pickle	Sound	Sight	Smell	Touch	Taste
	snap	long	strong	bumpy	sour

Grouping Details

Look at the paragraph about the fair again. It gives details about some of the senses. When you write a description, you should use words that tell about as many of the senses as you can.

Putting a Description Together

You can use the details from your chart to write a main-idea sentence and detail sentences. Liz wrote this main-idea sentence and detail sentences about the pickles.

Pickles are fun to eat.
They are bumpy. They taste sour.

Guided Practice:
Writing a Descriptive Paragraph

Study your chart of descriptive details. Then, write a main-idea sentence and detail sentences.

Checklist: Descriptive Writing

Complete this checklist.

CHECKLIST

✔ ■ Purpose and audience
✔ ■ Sentence that tells the main idea
✔ ■ Descriptive details
   ■ Sound   ■ Sight   ■ Smell

■ _____

■ _____

THINKING AND WRITING: Clustering

You know that a descriptive paragraph uses descriptive details. In order to write a clear description, you must decide which details to include. One way to do this is **clustering**.

First, write your topic and circle it. Near the circle write words that tell about your topic. Circle each word. Draw a line from each circle to your topic.

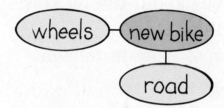

Here is a cluster that Ed made to find ideas for a descriptive paragraph about a bicycle he wanted. The circles and lines show how the ideas go together.

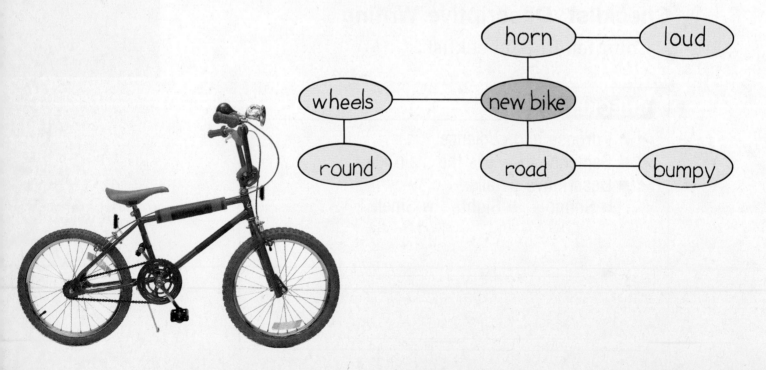

Thinking Like a Writer

■ What descriptive details do you think Ed should use?

Ed will choose details to describe the wheels, the horn, and the seat. He will not write about the road. That does not tell about the bicycle.

When you write a description, make a cluster to help you choose descriptive details.

THINKING APPLICATION Clustering

Here are some things that Ed's classmates said they wished they had. Think about how each one looks, feels, and sounds. Then pick one thing and make a cluster for it.

toy drum

train set

radio

toy robot

3 INDEPENDENT WRITING: A Description

Prewrite: Step 1

A descriptive paragraph should have a main-idea sentence and descriptive details.

Rita wanted to write about a special toy that her friends might like to have. Here is how she chose a topic.

Choosing a Topic

First, Rita wrote a list of things she wished she could have.

Next, she thought about each thing.

Last, she decided which thing to describe.

> a new kite
> roller skates
> toy animal ← Tell about one that talks.

Rita decided to describe a special kind of toy animal. She explored her topic by making a cluster.

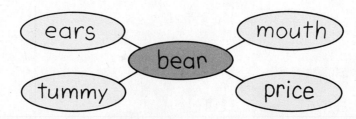

Exploring Ideas: Clustering Strategy

Rita thought about her **audience,** or who would read her description. She was writing her description for her friends. She wanted to be sure to tell them all about the toy bear.

Before she began to write, Rita closed her eyes and imagined the bear. Then, she made some changes in her cluster.

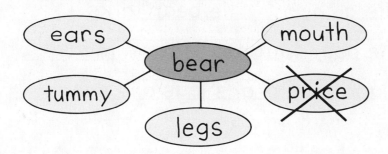

Thinking Like a Writer
- What did Rita add?
- What did Rita take out? Why?

YOUR TURN

Think of something you would like to describe. Use **Pictures** or your journal for ideas. Follow these steps.

- Make a list of things.
- Choose the one you like best.
- Make a cluster.
- Change your cluster if necessary.
- Think about your purpose and audience.

Write a First Draft: Step 2

Rita made a checklist so that she could write a first draft of her paragraph.

Here is Rita's first draft.

> The bear's brown ears are softest than cotton. Its mouth is like a cherry the bear talks. The bear laughs. Its tummy is round. The bear's legs are short.

Rita knew she could correct mistakes after she put all her ideas on paper.

YOUR TURN

Write a first draft for a paragraph that describes something you wish you could have. Ask yourself these questions.

■ What will my audience want to know?
■ How can I best use descriptive details?

⏱ **TIME-OUT** You might want to take some time out before you revise. Think about what you want to change.

Revise: Step 3

After she finished her first draft, Rita read it over to herself. Then, she shared her writing with a classmate. She wanted some ideas for making her paragraph better.

I like your paragraph, but I would like to know more about the bear's face.

I will add more details.

Next, Rita looked back at her planning checklist to make sure her paragraph was complete. She put a check next to the step that she forgot. She now has a checklist to use as she revises.

Rita revised her paragraph. She did not worry about the small mistakes she made. She knew she could correct them later.

Revising Checklist
- Remember purpose and audience.
- Write a sentence that tells the main idea.
- ✔ Add descriptive details.

Here is Rita's revised paragraph.

The toy I wish for is a talking bear. The bear's brown ears are softest than cotton. Its mouth is ^{tiny} like a cherry the bear talks. ^{and} The bear laughs. Its tummy is round. The bear's legs are short. ^{furry}

WISE
WORD
CHOICE

Thinking Like a Writer

- What descriptive words did Rita add?
- Do you think Rita's changes made her paragraph better? Why or why not?

YOUR TURN

Read your paragraph. Ask yourself these questions. Then revise your paragraph.

- Can any of my sentences be combined?
- Can I add descriptive words to make my writing clearer?

Proofread: Step 4

Rita knew she had to proofread her paragraph before it was complete. She used this proofreading checklist.

Here is part of Rita's proofread paragraph.

The toy I wish for is a talking bear.
The bear's brown ears are
softer
softest than cotton. Its mouth is
tiny
like a cherry. the bear talks. and

YOUR TURN

Proofreading Practice

Proofread this paragraph. Use proofreading marks to correct the mistakes. Then write the paragraph correctly on a separate piece of paper.

> I wish I had a guitar. The Guitar I want has the smoother wood of them all. The strings are long and thin It has a orange case.

Proofreading Checklist
- Did I indent my paragraph?
- Did I use capital letters correctly?
- Did I use the correct end marks?

Applying Your Proofreading Skills

Now proofread the descriptive paragraph you wrote. Read your checklist again. Then review **The Grammar Connection** and **The Mechanics Connection.** Use proofreading marks to correct your mistakes.

THE GRAMMAR CONNECTION

Remember these rules about comparing with adjectives.

■ Add **er** to an adjective to compare two nouns.

   Gus is tall**er** than Rita.

■ Add **est** to an adjective to compare more than two nouns.

   Nick is the tall**est** of all.

THE MECHANICS CONNECTION

Remember this rule about using commas with names of places.

■ Use a comma between the names of a city and a state.

   Jamestown, Virginia

Proofreading Marks

∧ Add
— Take out
≡ Make a capital letter
/ Make a small letter

Publish: Step 5

Rita wanted to share her description with her classmates. She copied her paragraph neatly. Then she read her paragraph aloud in class. Some of her classmates wanted to know more about the bear.

YOUR TURN

Make a final copy of your descriptive paragraph for your classmates. Use your best handwriting. Here are some other ways to share your paragraph.

SHARING SUGGESTIONS

Draw a picture to go with your paragraph. Put your paragraph and your picture on the bulletin board.	Tape record your paragraph. Then listen to your paragraph and the paragraphs of others.	Ask someone in your family to read your paragraph. Ask that person if he or she ever wished for the same thing.

4 SPEAKING AND LISTENING: Giving a Description

You can use what you know about writing a descriptive paragraph to give a short talk that describes something.

First, write the most important details about the thing you will describe.

NOTES: Birthday Party Wish
1. happy friends
2. crisp peanuts
3. noisy games
4. colored wrapping, ribbons

Then, use these guidelines for your talk.

> **SPEAKING GUIDELINES:** Giving a Description
>
> 1. Tell the main idea.
> 2. Use descriptive details.
> 3. Make a note card to help you practice your talk.
> 4. Speak in a loud, clear voice.

- Why is it important to speak clearly?
- How do descriptive details help my audience?

SPEAKING APPLICATION Giving a Description

Think of a party you wish to have. Make a note card to prepare a short talk about it for your classmates. The speaking guidelines will help you with your talk.

Use the guidelines below when you listen to your classmates give their talks.

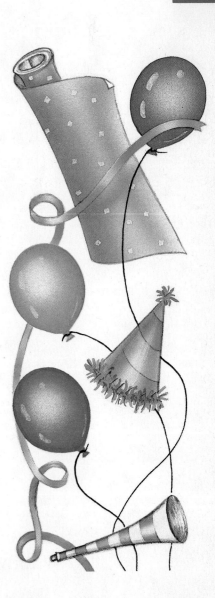

> **LISTENING GUIDELINES:** Giving a Description
>
> 1. Look at the person who is talking.
> 2. Listen for descriptive details so you can "see" what is being described.
> 3. Ask questions after the talk is over.

5 WRITER'S RESOURCES:
More About the Dictionary

Clear and exact words make your description interesting. A dictionary can help you find the words you need when you write.

You have learned that a dictionary gives word meanings. Some words have more than one meaning.

watch

1. to look or to look at.

2. A small timepiece that is worn on the wrist or that is carried in a pocket.

Notice that the word **watch** has more than one meaning. How many meanings are shown for the word **watch?**

Use the dictionary entry on the opposite page. Write 1 or 2 to tell which meaning of **watch** fits each sentence.

1. I watch Mom buy Dad a present. _____

2. His old watch has a broken strap. _____

3. Mom buys a new gold watch for Dad. _____

4. Then, we go to watch a movie. _____

5. I wish I had a new watch, too. _____

WRITING APPLICATION The Dictionary

Read this dictionary entry. Then use the word **pet** to write two sentences. Write a sentence for each meaning of the word.

pet
1. an animal that is fed, loved, and cared for by a person.
2. to stroke or to pat gently and with love.

THE CURRICULUM CONNECTION

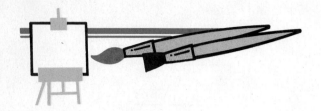

Writing About Art

When you think of art, you probably think of a painting or a drawing. But art can also be a statue, a photograph, or even a beautiful piece of woven cloth. When you look at a work of art, you use your senses to enjoy it.

ACTIVITIES

Picture Art
Think of a work of art that you have seen in a museum or in a book. Close your eyes and "see" the work of art in your mind. Talk about the work of art in class.

Describe Art
Look at the painting by Winslow Homer on the opposite page. What might the boy be wishing? Write a description of the painting for someone who has never seen it.

Respond to Literature
When we look at a picture or painting, we often dream about doing something special. Read this poem by Kate Greenaway. Then, write a paragraph telling where you would go if you had your own ship.

Waiting for Dad by Winslow Homer

When You and I Grow Up

When you and I
Grow up—Polly—
    I mean that you and me,
Shall go sailing in a big ship
    Right over all the sea.
                    —Kate Greenaway

UNIT CHECKUP

LESSON 1

Group Writing: A Description (page 206)   Read this main-idea sentence. Then, using descriptive details, write two detail sentences about the sentence.

I baked a loaf of bread.

LESSON 2

Thinking: Clustering (page 208)   Think of a pet you wish you could have. Use descriptive details to make a cluster about the pet.

LESSON 3

Writing a Description (page 210)   Use the cluster that you made about a pet to write a description.

LESSON 4

Speaking and Listening (page 218)   Ned plans to give a short talk to describe his school. Circle the rules he should follow.
- Use descriptive details.
- Speak softly.
- State the main idea.

LESSON 5

More About the Dictionary (page 220)   Circle the correct dictionary meaning of **bright** as it is used in this sentence.

Joey is a **bright** student.
- giving a lot of light, shining
- very smart or clever

THEME PROJECT *WHEN I GROW OLD*

You have learned to describe things in a paragraph. A poem can describe things, too.

Read this poem. Talk about the poem with your classmates. What words does the poet use to describe Grandma Lee? How do you think the poet feels about Grandma Lee?

Growing Old

When I grow old I hope to be
As beautiful as Grandma Lee.
Her hair is soft and fluffy white.
Her eyes are blue and candle bright.
And down her cheeks are cunning piles
Of little ripples when she smiles.

—Rose Henderson

Do you ever think about growing old? Whom do you hope you will look like?
- Write a short poem that describes that person.
- Draw a picture to go with your poem.

UNIT 9

Pronouns

JOURNAL

Come and ride around the block with me.
I'll bump a curb.
You bump a knee.

Karla Kuskin
from "12"

WHAT IS A PRONOUN?

A pronoun is a word that takes the place of a noun or nouns.

You and **I** are pronouns you often use. The pronoun **I** is always a capital letter.

Which words do these pronouns replace?

she   **he**   **they**   **it**   **we**

Amy   Al   Amy and Al   book   Al and I

 Replace each underlined word or words with a pronoun. Then write the sentence.

Example: <u>The children</u> play.   *They play.*

1. <u>Ann and Rick</u> are best friends.

_____

2. <u>Ann</u> writes a story.

_____

3. <u>Rick</u> draws a picture for the story.

_____

4. <u>The story</u> is about good friends.

_____

Extra Practice, page 241

WRITING APPLICATION A Story

Write a paragraph that tells how to make a gift for a friend. Use time-order words.

GRAMMAR: Pronouns   You may wish to have the children orally supply the pronouns.

2 USING *I* AND *ME*

Use **I** and **me** when you talk about yourself.

Use **I** in the subject part of a sentence. Use **me** after an action verb.

Jay and **I** help our neighbor.
Mrs. Dunn thanks Jay and **me**.

Name yourself last when you talk about yourself and another person.

Which pronoun goes before the verb? Which pronoun goes after it?

 Write **I** or **me** to complete each sentence.

Example: My friend and ___ work.   *I*

1. Bill and ___ see our neighbor.

2. Mrs. Santos likes Bill and ___.

3. Bill and ___ clean her yard.

4. Mrs. Santos calls Bill and ___.

5. Bill and ___ wave to her.

Extra Practice, page 241

 **WRITING APPLICATION** A Paragraph

Write a paragraph that tells how you might help a neighbor. Use the pronouns **I** and **me**.

GRAMMAR

3 USING *WE* AND *US*

Use **we** and **us** when you talk about yourself and another person.

Use **we** in the subject part of the sentence.
Use **us** after an action verb.

Tad and I hug the baby.   **We** hug the baby.
Ali hugs **Tad and me**.   Ali hugs **us**.

Which pronoun goes before the verb?

Which one goes after it?

 Circle the word that correctly replaces the underlined words in each sentence.

Example: <u>My brother and I</u> have a baby sister.
(We, Us)

1. <u>Rico and I</u> sing to Maria. (We, Us)
2. Maria smiles at <u>Rico and me</u>. (we, us)
3. <u>Rico and I</u> are Maria's friends. (We, Us)
4. <u>Rico and I</u> give Maria a bath. (We, Us)
5. Maria splashes <u>Rico and me</u>. (we, us)

Extra Practice, page 242

WRITING APPLICATION A Descriptive Paragraph

Write a paragraph to describe how you might make a baby sister or brother your friend. Use the pronouns **we** and **us**.

   Remind the children to name themselves last when they talk about themselves and another person.

4 USING PRONOUNS WITH VERBS

Pronouns and verbs work together the same way that nouns and verbs do.

Add **s** to most action verbs in the present when you use the pronouns **he**, **she**, and **it**.

Kay reads to Ned. **She** reads to Ned.

Do not add **s** to an action verb in the present when you use the pronouns **I**, **we**, **you**, and **they**.

Kay and I read to Ned. **We** read to Ned.

When do you add **s** to a verb?

 Tell which verb completes each sentence.

Example: She (call, calls) her friends.
    calls

1. I (visit, visits) Ned and Wilma.
2. We (sing, sings) songs together.
3. He (tell, tells) me a story.
4. It (make, makes) me laugh.
5. They (say, says) I am a good friend.

REMEMBER

- Add **s** to most action verbs in the present when you use the pronouns **he**, **she**, and **it**.
- Do not add **s** to most action verbs in the present when you use the pronouns **I**, **we**, **you**, and **they**.

 Choose the verb to finish each sentence correctly. Then write the sentence.

Example: You (know, knows) our friend Polly.
You know our friend Polly.

6. We (spend, spends) the day with Polly.

_____

- -

_____

7. She (call, calls) us her best friends.

_____

- -

_____

8. I (look, looks) at an old picture.

_____

- -

_____

9. It (show, shows) Polly and her sister.

_____

- -

_____

Extra Practice, Practice Plus, pages 242–244

COOPERATIVE
LEARNING

WRITING APPLICATION A Story

Write a story about visiting a friend like Ned or Polly. Then, have a partner circle the pronouns in your story.

5 MECHANICS: Contractions

Some pronouns and verbs can be put together to make contractions.

A **contraction** is a short form of two words. An **apostrophe** ' takes the place of the letters that are left out.

I am   he is   she is   they are   we are   you are

↓   ↓   ↓   ↓   ↓   ↓

I'm   he's   she's   they're   we're   you're

Which letter does each apostrophe replace?

 Write the contraction for the underlined words in each sentence.

Example: <u>She is</u> walking her dog.   *She's*

1. <u>We are</u> happy to have pets.

- - - - - - - - - - - - - - - - - -

2. <u>They are</u> our best friends.

- - - - - - - - - - - - - - - - - -

3. <u>You are</u> serving milk to your cat.

- - - - - - - - - - - - - - - - - -

4. <u>He is</u> giving his dog a bone.

- - - - - - - - - - - - - - - - - -

Extra Practice, page 245

 WRITING APPLICATION A Story

Write a story about an animal you would like to have as a friend. Use contractions in your story.

6 VOCABULARY BUILDING: Homophones

Some words sound alike but have different spellings and meanings.

Two friends write **to** each other.
She needs **four** stamps **for** the letter.

Choose the word to finish each sentence correctly. Then write the sentence.

Example: I bought (ate, eight) stamps.
I bought eight stamps.

1. My pen pal lives near the (sea, see).

- -

2. We (right, write) letters.

- -

3. I (no, know) Paco's address.

- -

4. I (would, wood) like to travel there.

- -

5. (Won, One) day I will visit him.

- -

Extra Practice, page 245

WRITING APPLICATION Vocabulary and Writing

COOPERATIVE LEARNING

Write a story about visiting a pen pal. Have a partner look for homophones in your story.

You may wish to have the children orally complete the sentences in the exercise.

GRAMMAR AND WRITING CONNECTION

Using Pronouns in Sentences

Use pronouns instead of repeating nouns.

Jill opened the box and filled the box.
Jill opened the box and filled **it**.

Both sentences tell what Jill did with the box. The first sentence sounds strange because it repeats **the box**. The second sentence makes more sense. It uses the pronoun **it** instead of **the box**.

COOPERATIVE
LEARNING

With your class look at the chart below. Tell the correct pronoun for each noun.

Example: Hal and Dorrie   *they*

Noun	Pronoun
1. Jill and Timmy	
2. Jill	
3. Timmy	
4. Mama and I	
5. house	

 Carl wrote these sentences when his friends moved away. Now he needs help revising them.

Write a pronoun for the words in ( ). Use words from the box. Then write the new sentences.

| I he she it we they |

Example: Carl said (Carl) was unhappy.
Carl said he was unhappy.

6. Jill and I were sad (Jill and I) were moving.

- -

7. Timmy said that (Timmy) would write to us.

- -

8. Jill knew that (Jill) would miss her friend.

- -

9. The movers said (the movers) were finished.

- -

10. Tim watched the van as (the van) left.

- -

Write a story about moving away from a good friend. Remember to use pronouns instead of repeating nouns.

GRAMMAR AND WRITING CONNECTION: Using Pronouns in Sentences

UNIT CHECKUP

LESSON 1

What Is a Pronoun? (page 228)   Match each noun with the correct pronoun.

1. the children — she
2. Tammy — it
3. the lamp — they

LESSON 2

Using I and me (page 229)   Write **I** or **me** to complete each sentence.

4. Ron and ___I___ work with our neighbor.

5. Miss Parks speaks with ___me___ .

6. She gives ___me___ some fruit.

LESSON 3

Using we and us (page 230)   Replace the underlined words with the pronoun **we** or **us**. Then write the sentence.

7. Pat and I dress our new baby brother.

We dress our new baby brother.

8. Joey likes to be with Pat and me.

Joey likes to be with us.

9. Pat and I give Joey some juice.

We give Joey some juice.

UNIT CHECKUP

Using Pronouns with Verbs (page 231)   Write the correct verb to finish each sentence.

10. We (know, knows) an old man. 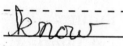 *know*

11. He (enjoy, enjoys) our visits. 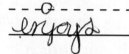 *enjoys*

12. I (give, gives) him a music box. *give*

LESSON 5

Mechanics: Contractions (page 233)   Write the contraction for the underlined words in each sentence.

13. I <u>am</u> building a house for my puppy. 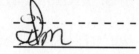 *I'm*

14. <u>You are</u> kind to help me. 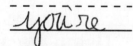 *you're*

15. <u>She is</u> lending us a hammer. *she's*

LESSON 6

Vocabulary Building: Homophones (page 234)   Circle the correct word to finish each sentence.

16. (Wood, Would) you like a pen pal?

17. I have a nice (won, one).

18. Hilda has (blue, blew) eyes.

WHO?

Play this game with a partner. Take turns telling about a special friend. Tell the person's name in the first sentence. Use pronouns in the other sentences to describe the person. Have your partner use your sentences to draw a picture of the person.

CONTRACTION CONNECTION

The pronoun **you** can be joined with **are** to make the contraction **you're. You're** sounds like the word **your,** but both words have different spellings and meanings.

You're a good friend.
You lend me **your** book.

Use **you're** or **your** to finish each sentence.

Example: _____ very kind.   You're very kind.

_____

1. _____ going to visit me.

2. Please bring _____ bicycle.

3. Where is _____ jacket?

4. I hope _____ having fun.

239

CREATIVE EXPRESSION

There are many ways to tell a friend your feelings. You can call your friend on the telephone. You can also write a letter, song, or poem. Read the poem below. How does the poet feel about the other person?

I
LIKE YOU

Although I saw you
The day before yesterday,
    And yesterday and today,
    This much is true—
I want to see you tomorrow, too!

—Masuhito (8th Century)

TRY IT OUT!

Think of someone you like very much. What is special about that person? Write a poem telling him or her how you feel. Use pronouns in your poem.

EXTRA PRACTICE

What Is a Pronoun? (page 228)   Write the pronoun that stands for each underlined word or words.

1. <u>Ryan and Jane</u> like music.   *We*

2. <u>Jane</u> plays the piano.   *She*

3. <u>You and I</u> clap.   *We*

4. I hear <u>a horn</u>.   *It*

5. <u>Ryan</u> plays for us.   *He*

Using *I* and *me* (page 229)   Write **I** or **me** to complete each sentence.

6. A neighbor calls Rosa and ___*I*___ .

7. ___*I*___ run to Mr. Tate.

8. Mr. Tate plays ball with ___*Me*___ .

9. ___*I*___ catch the ball.

10. Mr. Tate likes Rosa and ___*I*___ .

Using *we* and *us* (page 230)   Replace the underlined words in each sentence with **we** or **us**.

11.   <u>Hal and I</u> give Dorrie her bottle.   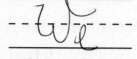 *We*

12.   Dorrie grins at <u>Hal and me</u>.   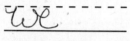 *Us*

13.   <u>Hal and I</u> pat Dorrie's head.   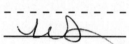 *We*

14.   Then <u>Hal and I</u> sing softly.   *We*

15.   Dorrie listens to <u>Hal and me</u>.   *Us*

Using Pronouns with Verbs (page 231)
Circle the verb that correctly completes each sentence.

16.   We (sit, sits) beside our old friend.
17.   She (show, shows) us how to bake bread.
18.   I (listen, listens) carefully.
19.   He (get, gets) the butter.
20.   It (melt, melts) quickly.

GRAMMAR

Additional practice for a difficult skill
Using Pronouns with Verbs (page 231)

A. Read each sentence. Circle the pronoun.
Then draw a line under the verb that
goes with the pronoun.

Example: They come at noon.
(They) <u>come</u> at noon.

21. (We) <u>walk</u> to Granny's house.
22. (She) <u>rests</u> in the garden.
23. (I) <u>water</u> the plants.
24. (He) <u>picks</u> some colorful flowers.
25. (They) <u>make</u> Granny smile.

B. Draw a line to match each pronoun
with the correct verb.

Example: They ▪ hear.
▪ hears.

26. I ▪ see.
▪ sees.

27. You ▪ jump.
▪ jumps.

28. She ▪ speak.
▪ speaks.

29. It ▪ break.
▪ breaks.

30. We ▪ paint.
▪ paints.

GRAMMAR

C. Choose the correct verb to finish each sentence. Then write the sentence.

31. I (dance, dances) with friends.

I dance with friends.

32. She (turn, turns) on the radio.

She turns on the radio.

33. It (sound, sounds) wonderful.

It sounds wonderful.

34. We (clap, claps) our hands.

We clap our hands.

35. He (kick, kicks) his feet.

He kicks his feet.

36. They (feel, feels) so happy.

They feel so happy.

Mechanics: Contractions (page 233)   Write the contraction for the underlined words in each sentence.

37. We are feeding our rabbits.   _We're_

38. They are our friends.   _They're_

39. She is filling the water bottle.   _She's_

40. I am chopping carrots.   _I'm_

41. You are kind to help me.   _you're_

Vocabulary Building: Homophones (page 234)
Circle the word that correctly completes the sentence.

42. (Where, Wear) does your pen pal live?
43. I (sea, see) the country on the map.
44. How often do you (write, right) to her?
45. (Wood, Would) you like to visit her?
46. What fun (to, two) travel far away!

UNIT
10

Writing a Letter

A book is inside me without my knowing it and then something—an experience or a remark—will trigger it off.

Aliki

AWARD
WINNING
SELECTION

What would you do if your best friend moved away? Read what happens to Robert when his friend Peter moves away.

We Are Best Friends
by Aliki

Peter came to tell Robert the news.

"I am moving away," he said.

"You can't move away," said Robert. "We are best friends."

"I am moving far away," said Peter.

"What will you do without me?" asked Robert. "Who will you play with?"

"We will live in a new house," said Peter.

"You will miss my birthday party!" said Robert.

"I will be going to a new school," said Peter.

"Who will you fight with?" asked Robert. "Nobody fights like best friends."

"I will make new friends," said Peter.

"You can't move away," said Robert. "You will miss me too much."

But Peter moved away. There was nothing to do without Peter. There was no one to play with. There was no one to share with. There was no one to fight with. Not the way best friends fight. There was no fun anymore.

"I'll bet Peter doesn't even remember me," said Robert. "It's a good thing he's not here. I'd have to punch him one."

"Hello. My name is Will," said a new face.
I don't like freckles, thought Robert.
"I used to go to another school," said Will.
I don't like glasses, thought Robert.
"My friends are all there," said Will.
I don't like silly names like Will, thought Robert.

"It was fun," said Will. "Not boring like this place."

A letter came for Robert. A letter from Peter.

Dear Robert,

I hope you still remember me. I like my new house now. I like my new school now. At first I didn't like anything. But now I have a friend, Alex. You are my best friend, but Alex is nice.

It is fun to have someone to play with again. It's not so lonely.

Love,
Peter

What does Peter say in his letter to let you know that he misses Robert?

Robert drew a letter. He drew two friends building a fort. He drew them playing with their cars. He drew them riding their bikes. He wrote: If you were here, this is what we'd be doing. But you're not.

Then he wrote: There is a new boy in school. He has freckles.

• • •

Robert saw Will by the fence.

"Did you lose something?" he asked.

"I thought I saw a frog," said Will.

"That's funny, looking for a frog," said Robert.

"What's funny about it? I like frogs," said Will. "I used to have a pet frog named Greenie. He'd wait for me by the pond near where I lived. He must miss me a lot."

"I know where there are frogs," said Robert. "Right in my garden."

"You're just saying that," said Will.

"I mean it," said Robert. "You can see for yourself."

"If I had a frog in my garden, I'd share it," said Will.

"That's what I'm doing," said Robert.

Robert and Will rode home together. They went straight into the garden. The frogs were there. One leaped under a bush, and Will caught it.

"I'll call you Greenie the Second," he said. "You like me already, don't you?"

"The frogs lay their eggs here every year," said Robert.

"It's almost time. My friend Peter used to come watch the tadpoles. He called them Inkywiggles. He'll miss them."

"Why?" asked Will.

"He moved away," said Robert. "Just about the time you came. I write him letters."

"Then you can write about the Inkywiggles," said Will.

They laughed.

"I haven't had so much fun since I moved here," said Will.

"Neither have I," said Robert.

Thinking Like a Reader

1. Think about how Robert feels when Peter moves away. Tell how Robert feels in a few sentences.

2. How would you feel if your best friend moved away?

Write your thoughts in your journal.

Thinking Like a Writer

3. How does the author let you know that Robert and Will are becoming friends?

4. How would you let the readers know that the friends are beginning to like each other?

Write your answers in your journal.

Brainstorm *Vocabulary*

When Peter wrote a letter to Robert, he used the words **remember, like, new,** and **first.** Write each word in your journal. Then, write an antonym for each word. Include any new words in a personal word list.

Talk It Over *Talk on the Telephone*

Work with a partner. Imagine that you are friends who live far away from each other. Imagine that you are talking to each other on the telephone. Talk about how you feel.

Quick Write *Write About a Picture*

In your journal draw a picture that you could send to a friend. Then, write sentences to your friend that tell about the picture.

Idea Corner *Think About Writing to Friends*

What might you write about in a letter to a friend? Write those ideas in your journal. You might make a list of people or draw pictures.

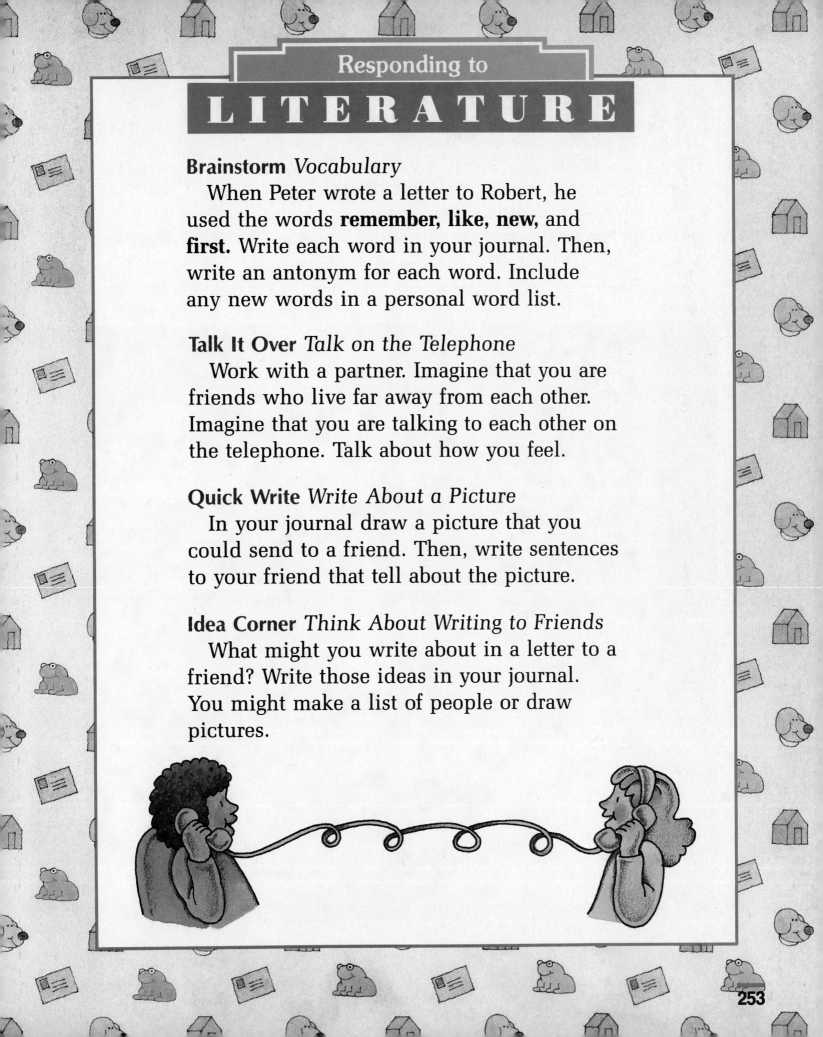

PICTURES

SEEING LIKE A WRITER

Finding Ideas for Writing
Look at the pictures. Think about what you see.
What ideas for writing letters do the pictures give you?
Write your ideas in your journal.

PICTURES: Ideas for Writing a Friendly Letter

COOPERATIVE LEARNING

1 GROUP WRITING: A Friendly Letter

The purpose of a letter is to share ideas with your **audience**. What things should you know before you write a letter?

- Parts of letters
- Kinds of letters

Parts of Letters

Notice the different parts of Jason's letter.

> 11 Park Road
> Macon, Georgia 31297
> May 3, 1990
>
> Dear Kendra,
>   I made a puppet in school today. It has a funny face. I will bring the puppet with me the next time I visit you.
>   Your friend,
>   Jason

Heading

Greeting

Body

Closing
Signature

Guided Practice: Parts of Letters

As a class, think about a letter that Kendra might write to Jason. Then, write each part of the letter.

Kinds of Letters

There are different kinds of letters. **Thank-you letters** thank someone for something. **Friendly letters** tell someone something interesting. When you write a letter think about why you are writing.

Putting a Friendly Letter Together

Here is how one class began the body of a letter that Kendra might write.

> I hope you can come to visit me soon.
> I would like to see your puppet.

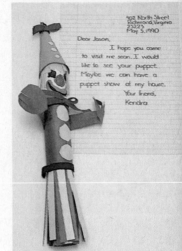

Guided Practice: Writing a Friendly Letter

Write a friendly letter to a friend. Include all parts of a letter.

Checklist: A Friendly Letter

A checklist will help you remember the parts of a letter. Complete this checklist.

CHECKLIST

- ✔ Purpose and audience
- ✔ Heading
- ✔ Greeting
- ✔ Body
  - ■ Tell about something interesting

- ✔ _____

- ✔ _____

2 THINKING AND WRITING: Solving Riddles

When you write a friendly letter, you can tell your reader something interesting. You might even write about something funny.

Carla plans to write a friendly letter to a pen pal. She wants to include something funny in her letter. Carla finds some riddles in a book. She makes a list of her favorite riddles.

Why do cows wear bells?
Because their horns don't work!

How can you tell if an elephant is nearby?
You can smell the peanuts on its breath!

What kind of dog always knows the time?

A watch dog!

Thinking Like a Writer

■ How are all of Carla's riddles alike?

Carla's riddles ask questions and have silly answers. Her riddles tell about animals.

THINKING APPLICATION Solving Riddles

Not all riddles ask questions. Here are some other riddles that Carla liked. Write the number of each riddle below the picture that solves it.

1. First you see me in the grass
   Dressed in yellow gay.
   Then I dress all in white
   Then I fly away.

2. You throw away the outside
      and cook the inside.
   Then you eat the outside
      and throw away the inside.

3. Red and blue, purple and green.
   No one can reach it,
   Not even a queen.

_____   _____   _____

- - - - - - -   - - - - - - -   - - - - - - -

_____   _____   _____

3 INDEPENDENT WRITING: A Friendly Letter

Prewrite: Step 1

A friendly letter has a **heading** and a **greeting**. It tells about something interesting in the **body**. A letter ends with a **closing** and a **signature**.

Here is how Mike chose a topic for a friendly letter to his friend Sara.

> my baby brother
>
> a good book
>
> Our new puppy ← This will interest Sara.

Choosing a Topic

First, Mike wrote a list of things that might be interesting to Sara.

Next, he asked himself questions about what Sara would want to know.

Last, he decided what to write about.

Here is a cluster that Mike made to show some ideas about his new puppy, Alf.

Exploring Ideas: Clustering Strategy

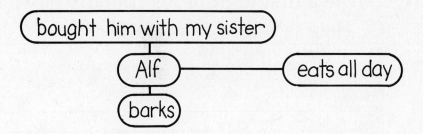

Mike thought about his puppy. Then he decided to change his cluster.

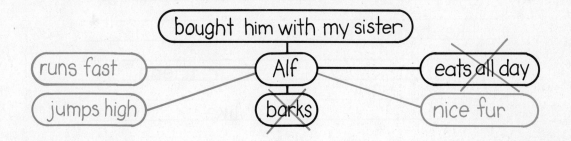

Thinking Like a Writer

- What did Mike add to his cluster?
- What did Mike take out? Why?

YOUR TURN

JOURNAL

Now, prepare to write your own letter. Use **Pictures** or your journal for ideas. Follow these steps.

- Choose a person to whom you will write.
- Choose one topic for the body.
- Make a cluster to explore topic ideas.
- Think about your purpose and audience.

Write a First Draft: Step 2

Mike made a checklist so that he could write a first draft of his friendly letter.

Here is Mike's first draft.

> dear Sara
>
>   My sister and me bought a dog. i named the dog Alf. Alf runs fast. Alf jumps high. He has a black nose. Dogs like bones. His fur is nice.
>
>   Your friend,
>   Mike

Planning Checklist
- Remember purpose and audience.
- Heading
- Greeting
- Body—tell about something interesting
- Closing
- Signature

YOUR TURN

Write a first draft for a friendly letter. Ask yourself these questions.

- What will my audience want to know?
- How can I make my letter interesting?

⏱ TIME-OUT Take some time out before you revise. Think about what you might change.

Revise: Step 3

After he finished his first draft, Mike read it over to himself. Then, he shared his writing with a classmate. He wanted some ideas for making his letter better.

Mike looked back at his planning checklist to make sure that his letter was complete. He put a check next to the step that he forgot. He now has a checklist to use as he revises.

Your letter is very nice. You should add a heading to make it complete.

I will. Thanks for your help.

Revising Checklist
- Remember purpose and audience.
✔ ■ Heading
- Greeting
- Body— tell about something interesting
- Closing
- Signature

Mike revised his letter. He did not correct small mistakes. He knew he could fix them later.

Here is Mike's revised letter.

15 Red Road
Dallas, Texas 75247
June 2, 1990

dear Sara

   My sister and me bought a dog. i
named the dog Alf. Alf runs fast. Alf
                          and
jumps high. He has a black nose. Dogs
               shiny
like bones. His fur is nice. I like to
               soft
pet Alf.
                    Your friend,

                    Mike

WISE
WORD
CHOICE

Thinking Like a Writer

- Which letter part did Mike add?
- Which sentences did he change? Why?

YOUR TURN

Read your first draft. Ask yourself these
questions. Then, revise your letter.

- Did I include all the parts of a letter?
- Do I need to add or take out a sentence?
- Can any of my sentences be combined?

Proofread: Step 4

Mike knew he had to proofread his friendly letter before it was complete. He used this proofreading checklist.

Here is part of Mike's proofread letter.

dear Sara,
____
    My sister and ~~me~~ bought a dog. i
named the dog Alf. Alf runs fast. *and* Alf

YOUR TURN

Proofreading Practice

Proofread this part of a letter. Use proofreading marks to correct the mistakes. Then write the letter correctly on a separate piece of paper.

> dear Mike,
>
>   My brother and me took our dog to the park. Us played catch with him.
>
>   Your friend
>   Sara

Proofreading Checklist
- Did I indent the body of the letter?
- Did I use commas in the correct places?
- Did I use capital letters correctly?
- Have I used the correct end marks?

Applying Your Proofreading Skills

Now proofread the friendly letter you wrote. Read your checklist again. Then review **The Grammar Connection** and **The Mechanics Connection.** Use proofreading marks to correct your mistakes.

THE GRAMMAR CONNECTION

Remember these rules about pronouns.
- Use **I** and **we** in the subject part of a sentence.
   I write a letter.
   We mail the letters.
- Use **me** and **us** after an action verb.
   You write to **me**.
   She writes to **us**.
- Always name yourself last.
   Granny writes to you and **me**.

Proofreading Marks

∧ Add

— Take out

≡ Make a capital letter

/ Make a small letter

THE MECHANICS CONNECTION

Remember these rules about commas in letters.
- Put a comma between the day and year in a date.
   March 3, 1990
- Put a comma after the greeting.
   Dear Wini,
- Put a comma after the closing.
   Your friend,

Publish: Step 5

Mike wanted to mail his letter. First, he neatly copied the letter. Then, he addressed an envelope. Last, he mailed the letter.

Mike Cagney
15 Red Road
Dallas, Texas 75247

Sara Cummings
499 Park Street
Mentor, Ohio 44060

YOUR TURN

Make a final copy of your letter. Use your best handwriting. Here are some other ways to share your letter.

SHARING SUGGESTIONS

Address an envelope for your letter. Then, mail your letter to the person to whom you wrote it.	Draw a picture of the person to whom you wrote your letter. Share your picture and letter with that person.	Make your own writing paper. Draw little pictures in the margins of lined paper. Copy your letter on the paper.

4 SPEAKING AND LISTENING: Taking a Telephone Message

One way to share your ideas with others is to talk on the telephone.

Sometimes people who call on the telephone want to leave a message. Here is a telephone message that Lea took for her brother, Jim.

October 6, 1990   4:00 P.M.

Jim,
    Your friend Tony called. His number is 555-5789. He wants you to play at his house tomorrow. Please call him back tonight.

                              Lea

Use these guidelines when you take a telephone message.

Guidelines for Taking a Telephone Message

1. Write the date and time of the call.
2. Write whom the message is for.
3. Write the caller's name and telephone number neatly.
4. Write the caller's message.
5. Sign your name on the message.

- Why is it important for me to write the date and time of the call?
- Why should I sign my name on the message?

Speaking Application Taking a Telephone Message

With a partner, make up a telephone conversation in which one of you leaves a message. Act out your conversation in class. Have your classmates write down the telephone message.

Use these speaking guidelines.

Guidelines for Talking on the Telephone

1. Give your name.
2. Name the person with whom you wish to speak.
3. Tell what message you want the person to get.
4. Leave your number.
5. Be polite.

5 WRITER'S RESOURCES: Using the Newspaper

When you write a friendly letter to someone, you might want to talk about things in the news. Use a newspaper to find out about the news.

A story in a newspaper usually answers questions called the five **W's—Who?**, **What?**, **Where?**, **When?**, and **Why?**

Read the newspaper story.

Students Clean Maple Park

by Karen Wong
The students of Village School will clean up Maple Park. The Park is between First Avenue and Broad Street. Work on the park will begin next month. The students said they want a clean park where they can play with their friends.

This newspaper story begins with a **headline**. A headline tells what the story is about. The name of the person who wrote the story comes after the headline.

 Look at the newspaper story again. Write the answers to the five **W** questions below.

1. Who? _____

_ _

_____

2. What? _____

_ _

_____

3. Where? _____

_ _

_____

4. When? _____

_ _

_____

5. Why? _____

_ _

_____

WRITING APPLICATION The Newspaper

Find a newspaper story that you like. Cut out the story and paste it on a piece of paper. Use the story to answer the five **W** questions.

Writing About Communications

You can share your thoughts with others in many ways. You can talk to someone on the telephone. You can also write someone a letter. You might use the newspaper, television, or the radio to share thoughts, too.

ACTIVITIES

Picture a Message Look in an old newspaper or magazine for an ad with a picture. Share the ad with your class. Tell how it makes you feel about the thing that is for sale.

Write a Message Write a friendly letter to someone about the ad you found. Try to get the person to feel the same way about the ad as you do.

Respond to Literature You can use all your senses to share your thoughts. The book Happy Birthday, Grampie by Susan Pearson tells how a girl makes a birthday card for her grandfather. Read the words from the book. How does the girl communicate with her grandfather? Write a paragraph that tells how to make a card like the one the girl made. Use time-order words. Then make the card.

> *Happy Birthday, Grampie*
>
> There. She was done. She held the card up, pleased with her work. This was one card Grampie would be able to "see" even though he was blind, because Martha had made it in a special way. Every part of it had a different feeling—the construction paper on the bottom, then the paper doily, then the piece of felt cut like a heart, and finally, the shiny, stick-on letters.

UNIT CHECKUP

LESSON 1

Group Writing: A Friendly Letter (page 256)
Draw a line to match each letter part with the word that describes it.

Your friend,   Body
I had fun at your party.   Closing
Dear Kevin,   Greeting

LESSON 2

Thinking: Solving Riddles (page 258)
On a separate piece of paper draw a picture about this riddle.

    I have a bark, but I am not a dog.

LESSON 3

Writing a Friendly Letter (page 260)

Write a letter to a friend about a funny riddle.

LESSON 4

Speaking and Listening (page 268)
Circle the sentence that would be in a telephone message.
1. Uncle Bill called at 3:00 P.M.
2. Thank you for your gift.

LESSON 5

Using the Newspaper (page 270)
On another piece of paper, write the five W questions that most newspaper stories answer.

THEME PROJECT STAMPS

You have learned to communicate with others by writing letters. Before you can mail a letter, you must put a stamp on the envelope.

Some stamps are special. They show a picture of an animal or a place. They may also show a picture of someone famous. These stamps help us remember the person, place, or thing.

Look at the stamps. Talk about them with your classmates. What does each one make us remember?

Make a stamp for a special friend.
- You can draw a picture of your friend on the stamp. You can also draw a picture of something your friend likes.
- Then, write your friend a letter that tells about the stamp.
- Give the stamp and letter to your friend.

UNIT

11

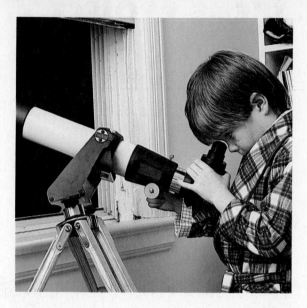

Adverbs

JOURNAL

You are a dancy little thing,
You are a rascal, star!
You seem to be so near to me,
And yet you are so far.

Gwendolyn Brooks
from "De Koven"

1 WHAT IS AN ADVERB?

An adverb tells more about a verb.

An adverb can tell **when**, **where**, or **how**.

Yesterday, Juan bought a telescope.

Does the adverb tell when, where, or how?

 Circle the verb in each sentence. Then write the adverb.

Example: Juan quickly opened the box.

Juan quickly (opened) the box.

quickly _____

- -

1. He slowly read the directions. _____

_____

- -

2. He looked up. _____

_____

- -

3. Soon Juan saw Mars. _____

_____

- -

4. He carefully took notes. _____

_____

- -

5. Juan later found Venus. _____

Extra Practice, page 291

WRITING APPLICATION A Story

Imagine that you have the biggest telescope in the world. Write a story about the things you can see with it. Circle the adverbs in your story.

You may wish to have the children orally complete the exercise.

2 ADVERBS THAT TELL *WHEN* AND *WHERE*

An adverb can tell **when** or **where**.

The astronauts fly **today**.
They wait **here**.

Which adverb tells when?
Which adverb tells where?

 Name the verb in each sentence. Then name the adverb. Tell if the adverb tells when or where.

Example: I always go to the space center.
    go (verb)   always (adverb)   when

1. The students come early.
2. They move forward.
3. Soon, they see two astronauts.
4. The astronauts move outside.
5. They stand nearby.

REMEMBER
- An **adverb** tells more about a verb.
- Some adverbs tell when or where.

 Circle the adverb in each sentence. Write **when** if it tells when. Write **where** if it tells where.

Example: Today, everyone is excited.

(Today,) everyone is excited.

when

_____

6. The astronauts go inside.

_____

7. They look around.

_____

8. Now, they check the radio.

_____

9. Finally, the astronauts are ready.

_____

10. The rocket zooms up.

Extra Practice, Practice Plus, pages 291–293

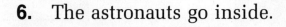

WRITING APPLICATION A Paragraph

Where do the astronauts fly? Use adverbs in writing a paragraph about their trip.

GRAMMAR: Adverbs That Tell When and Where   Have the children orally name the adverbs in their stories.

3 ADVERBS THAT TELL *HOW*

Some adverbs tell **how**.

Today, the space ranger spoke **quietly**.

Which adverb tells how the ranger spoke?

 Circle the verb in each sentence. Then write the adverb that tells how.

Example: The captain worked bravely.
The captain (worked) bravely.
bravely

1. The space station bell rang loudly. _____

2. Dale walked quickly to the computer. _____

3. Suki watched closely. _____

4. The captain proudly thanked her crew. _____

Extra Practice, page 294

COOPERATIVE
LEARNING

WRITING APPLICATION A Letter

Imagine that you are on a space station. Write a letter to a classmate about being there. Then exchange letters. Circle the adverbs in each other's work.

MECHANICS: Writing Titles

Begin the first word of a book title with a capital letter.
Use capital letters to begin each important word in the title.
Underline all the words in the title of a book.

I read a book called <u>Astronauts in Space</u>.

Which words in the title begin with a capital letter?

 Write each book title correctly.

Example: a rocket to adventure

A Rocket to Adventure

1. space dangers

---

2. air and space

---

3. visiting the moon

---

4. women in space

---

5. life on mars

Extra Practice, page 294

COOPERATIVE
LEARNING

WRITING APPLICATION A List

List the titles of several of your favorite books. Share your list with a classmate. Check each other's lists to see that you have written your titles correctly.

Have the children create a class list of favorite books.

5 VOCABULARY BUILDING: Suffixes

A **suffix** is a word part that is added to the end of a word. A suffix changes the meaning of a word.

Suffix	Meaning	Example
less	without	care + less = care**less**
ful	full of	help + ful = help**ful**

What does **less** mean?   What does **ful** mean?

 Tell which word in each sentence has a suffix. Then tell what the word means.

Example: The space trip was wonderful.
wonderful   full of wonder

1. The young explorer was weightless.
2. He was fearful when he floated upward.
3. Dick had to be careful.
4. He was hopeful as he neared the ship.
5. He did not feel helpless.

REMEMBER
- A **suffix** is a word part that is added to the end of a word.
- The suffix **less** means "without."
- The suffix **ful** means "full of."

Add **ful** or **less** to the word in ( ). Then write the new word.

Example: The clean spaceship is (spot).
spotless

6. The (fear) astronaut likes adventures.

7. Dina smiles because she feels (joy).

8. She meets friendly and (peace) people.

9. The clean planet is (spot).

10. The red and green plants are (color).

Extra Practice, page 294

WRITING APPLICATION Vocabulary and Writing

Imagine that you are a space explorer who has found a new planet. Write a letter home about what you found there. Use words with the suffixes **ful** and **less**.

VOCABULARY: Suffixes   Have the children explain the meaning of each new word they make.

GRAMMAR AND WRITING CONNECTION

Using Adverbs in Sentences

Use adverbs to make your writing more exact.

The astronaut looked.
Yesterday, the astronaut looked carefully.

Name the adverbs that tell **when** and **how** the action takes place.

COOPERATIVE LEARNING

With your class look at the chart. Read each verb. Write three different adverbs for each verb.

verb	Adverbs		
	how	where	when
fly	*quickly*	*there*	*now*
land			
speak			
work			

Rewrite each sentence. Add an adverb from the word box, or think of an adverb of your own.

soon	slowly	yesterday	quickly	calmly	outside
around	behind	carefully	last	finally	inside

Example: The astronauts spoke.
The astronauts spoke softly.

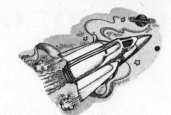

1. The spaceship flew.

_____

- -

_____

2. The astronauts watched the stars.

_____

- -

_____

3. They landed on the moon.

_____

- -

_____

4. The spaceship door opened.

_____

- -

_____

5. The astronauts walked.

_____

- -

_____

Read this story starter. Then finish the story. Use adverbs to make your sentences more exact.

I will never forget the exciting week I spent on the moon with my robot Robo.

GRAMMAR AND WRITING CONNECTION: Using Adverbs in Sentences

UNIT CHECKUP

LESSON 1

What Is an Adverb? (page 278)   Circle the adverb in each sentence.

1. Carl happily looked at Mars.
2. Later, he spotted Jupiter.
3. A comet flew by.
4. Linda quickly went to the window.
5. She looked up.

LESSON 2

Adverbs That Tell *When* and *Where* (page 279)
Circle the adverb in each sentence. Write **when** if it tells when. Write **where** if it tells where.

6. Today, the rocket leaves. _____

7. The astronauts stand nearby. _____

8. Now, they board the ship. _____

9. They sit inside. _____

LESSON 3

Adverbs That Tell *How* (page 281)   Circle the adverb that tells **how**.

10. The space station moved quickly.
11. The captain calmly looked outside.
12. He quietly gave an order.
13. A spaceship passed silently.
14. The astronauts waved happily.

UNIT CHECKUP

Mechanics: Writing Titles (page 282)   Circle each book title that is written correctly.

15. the first Space Trip

The First Space Trip

16. Orbits Unknown

orbits unknown

17. The Planets We See

The Planets We See

18. Frankie Flies to the Moon

Frankie Flies To The Moon

LESSON 5

Vocabulary Building: Suffixes (page 283)   Add **ful** or **less** to the word in (   ). Then write the new word.

19. I am (fear) that I am lost. _____

20. My broken radio is (use). _____

21. I will be (thank) to return home. _____

22. The captain is kind and (thought). _____

23. His clean spaceship is (spot). _____

SPACE STATION

Work with a partner. Add **ly** to each word in the spaceship. The new word will be an **adverb** that tells how. Use the new words to tell each other about a vacation on a space station.

slow   quiet   neat

loud   quick

SUFFIX CREATURES

Meet the suffix space creatures. They use a suffix in every sentence they say. Use **ful** or **less** to finish each sentence about these creatures.

1. We are color _____ green people.

2. Zot and Zim are hair _____ .

3. We are kind and thought _____ .

SKY ROCKETS

Draw a big rocket on a piece of paper. In the rocket write a sentence that uses an adverb. Then, cut out your rocket. Attach a string to your rocket. Hang it from the ceiling.

CREATIVE EXPRESSION

Many poems have words that **rhyme**. Rhyming words end with the same sound. They make the poem pleasing to hear. Read this poem. Name the words that rhyme.

Oh, it will be fine
To rocket through space
And see the reverse
Of the moon's dark face,

To travel to Saturn
Or Venus or Mars,
Or maybe discover
Some uncharted stars.

—Frances Frost
from "Valentine for Earth"

TRY IT OUT! JOURNAL

Imagine that you borrow a rocket ship. Write a poem that tells where you will go. Use adverbs and words that rhyme.

EXTRA PRACTICE

What Is an Adverb? (page 278)   Circle the adverb in each sentence.

1. Sometimes we go to the space museum.
2. Nina and I look around.
3. Today, a man shows us the planets.
4. We listen quietly.
5. We like it here.
6. I always learn something.
7. I read the signs carefully.
8. Now, I read about rockets.

Adverbs That Tell *When* and *Where* (page 279) Circle the adverb in each sentence. Write **when** if the adverb tells when. Write **where** if the adverb tells where.

9. Yesterday, we watched a lift-off. _Yesterday_

10. Many people were there. _there_

11. Then, the countdown began. _then_

12. We looked up. _up_

13. The rocket flew nearby. _nearby_

14. Soon, the rocket will return. _soon_

Additional practice for a difficult skill

Adverbs That Tell _When_ and _Where_ (page 279)

A. Read the adverbs in the box. Write each adverb in the correct part of the chart.

often	around	nearby
then	away	always

15.

When	Where
often	

B. Circle the correct adverb to complete each sentence.

16. (Today, Across) is my birthday.

17. All my friends are (then, here).

18. We sit (yesterday, quietly).

19. It is sunny (outside, late).

20. (Soon, Far) we feel hungry.

21. We eat (never, nearby).

22. A plane flies (above, yesterday).

23. We look (early, up).

C. Write an adverb to complete each sentence. The word in ( ) tells which kind of adverb to write. Use the words in the box.

Example: We (when) think about space trips.
We often think about space trips.

finally outside down today around often

24. We pretend to be astronauts (when).

_____

- -

_____

25. Lu and I fly (where).

_____

- -

_____

26. I look (where).

_____

- -

_____

27. We (when) reach the moon.

_____

- -

_____

28. Lu and I step (where).

_____

- -

_____

Adverbs That Tell _How_ (page 281)   Read each sentence. Circle the adverb that tells how.

29.   I work carefully in the space station.

30.   I softly call the captain.

31.   George calmly goes to the computer.

Mechanics: Writing Titles (page 282)   Circle each book title that is written correctly.

32.   stars in the sky   <u>Stars in the Sky</u>

33.   <u>The Secret Moon</u>   The Secret Moon

34.   <u>Jupiter and Mars</u>   <u>Jupiter and mars</u>

35.   <u>our star</u>   <u>Our Star</u>

36.   <u>Robby Robot</u>   Robby Robot

Vocabulary Building: Suffixes (page 283) Circle the suffix that correctly completes each word in (   ).

37.   Space explorers are (wonder).
(ful, less)

38.   These brave people are (fear).
(ful, less)

39.   Astronauts are (weight) in space.
(ful, less)

40.   An astronaut must be (care).
(ful, less)

41.   A rocket should be (spot).
(ful, less)

MAINTENANCE

Units 1, 3, 5, 7, 9, 11

Unit 1: Sentences
Statements and Questions, Commands and Exclamations (pages 3, 5, 7) Read each sentence. Is it a **statement**, a **question**, a **command**, or an **exclamation**? Write which kind of sentence it is.

1. What a great city this is! _____

2. Have you lived here a long time? _____

3. Please follow me. _____

4. You will like my apartment. _____

Beginning and Ending Sentences (page 13)
Circle the correct end mark for each sentence.

5. Come to the city hall   .   !
6. Who will be there   !   ?
7. Our mayor will visit today   .   ?
8. How interesting this is   ?   !

Unit 3: Nouns
Special Nouns (pages 63, 65)   Write each sentence correctly.

9. My sister mara likes pet shows.

- -

10. She brings her cat kippy.

- -

11. There is a show in january.

- -

More Than One
More Words for More Than One (pages 67, 69)
Write each noun to name more than one.

12. fence

- - - - - - - - - - - - - - - - - -

13. bus

- - - - - - - - - - - - - - - - - -

14. wish

- - - - - - - - - - - - - - - - - -

15. child

- - - - - - - - - - - - - - - - - -

Unit 5: Verbs
Verbs That Tell About the Present
Verbs That Tell About the Past (pages 115, 117)
Circle the correct verb.

16. Yesterday, Jan (calls, called) me.
17. We (wants, wanted) to have a party.
18. Now, I (greet, greeted) my friends.

Using *be*
Using *do* and *see* (pages 119, 121) Circle the correct verb.

19. Yesterday (is, was) Valentine's Day.
20. Now, I (see, sees) hearts everywhere.
21. You (does, did) not make a card.

Using *come*, *go*, and *run* (page 122) Circle the correct verb.

22. I (goes, went) to the garden.
23. Now, Mama (comes, come) outside.
24. I (run, runs) to her with flowers.

Using *give* and *sing* Using *have* and *has*
(pages 123, 124) Circle the correct verb.

25. Yesterday, I (give, gave) Dad a tie.
26. Now, Jan (have, has) a mug for him.
27. We (sing, sings) a happy song.

Unit 7: Adjectives
What Is an Adjective? (page 176) Read each sentence. Then circle the adjective.

28. There is a well in the little park.
29. Yoko tosses old coins into it.
30. She wishes for several pets.

Adjectives That Compare (page 179) Circle **er** or **est** to complete the adjective in ( ).

31. Tim wants to be (fast) than Sara is. (er, est)
32. Walt hopes to be the (young) swimmer. (er, est)
33. Stan tried to be (strong) than I am. (er, est)

Unit 9: Pronouns

What Is a Pronoun? (page 228)   Replace each underlined word or words with a pronoun. Then write the pronoun.

34.   Sue and Mario want to build a boat.

_____

35.   Sue finds the tools.

_____

Using *I* and *me* (page 229)   Write **I** or **me** to complete each sentence.

36.   _____ hold baby Kira.

37.   Kira gives her shoes to _____ .

Using *we* and *us* (page 230)   Replace the underlined words with **we** or **us**.

38.   Our neighbors like Len and me.   _____

39.   Len and I water their plants.   _____

Using Pronouns with Verbs (page 231)   Circle the correct verb to finish each sentence.

40. We (talk, talks) with an old man.
41. He (take, takes) us to his pond.
42. I (see, sees) three ducks.

Unit 11: Adverbs

What Is an Adverb? (page 278)   Circle the adverb in each sentence.

43. I go outside.
44. Next, I study a space map.
45. I carefully look for each planet.

Adverbs That Tell *When* and *Where*

(page 279)   Circle the adverb in each sentence. Write **when** if it tells when. Write **where** if it tells where.

46. The rocket left early.   _____

47. The astronauts looked outside.   _____

Adverbs That Tell *How* (page 281)   Circle the adverb that tells **how**.

48. The space station moves smoothly.
49. The space rangers work happily.
50. The captain speaks gently to them.

UNIT
12

Writing a
Book Report

Sun and sky and bumblebee,
This book I hold belongs to me.
Grass and leaves and shady tree,
This book I read belongs to me.
Cliffs and clouds and distant sea,
This book belongs to me, to me!

Arnold Lobel

Imagine that you have a friend from outer space! Read about the fun that these friends from two very different worlds have with each other.

The Blue Rocket Fun Show or, Friends Forever

by Thomas P. Lewis

Leslie and Niki were new best friends. Niki had come to the city, just for the summer, with the Blue Rocket Fun Show. She lived in the park in a bug-like house, next to all the animals and the rides.

Leslie and Niki did everything together. They both liked movies and books about rocket ships and stars and faraway planets up in the sky. They saw movies like <u>Star Wars</u>, <u>Supergirl</u>, and <u>E.T.</u> over and over again.

At night, when there were no clouds, they went to the roof of Leslie's apartment building. Leslie brought her telescope. Up close, the moon looked like the skin of a silver orange.

"The dark parts are called seas," Niki said. "But there is no water in them."

They found the Big Dipper, which looked like a cooking pan floating through the sky. The Big Dipper was made of seven stars. It seemed to point to another star.

"That is Polaris, the North Star," Niki said. "It is really **three** stars. They are so close together they look like one."

Niki and Leslie had sleep-overs almost every night. Sometimes they slept at Leslie's, and sometimes they slept at Niki's.

Niki did not sleep on a regular bed. She slept on pillows inside a jar-like thing. There was plenty of room there for Leslie, too, and their dolls and stuffed animals. Part of the jar was a screen. They could watch TV shows inside the jar.

How does the author use details to let you "see" the special things that Niki and Leslie do at night?

"I hope we stay friends forever," Leslie said.

"Me, too," Niki said.

• • •

Only one thing made Leslie sad.

"When will you go away, Niki?" she asked.

"Soon," said Niki.

"I will miss you," Leslie said.

"I will miss you, too."

"I want to write to you," Leslie said. "But I don't know where you live."

"I . . . I . . . it is very far away," Niki said.

One day Niki said, "I am not supposed to tell. But you are my best friend. We are going away tonight."

"Oh!" said Leslie.

"Leslie, there is something else I want to tell you. But it is very hard. I . . . I don't want you to be afraid of me."

"Best friends aren't afraid when they are together," Leslie said.

"I'm not like you," Niki said. "I am not a human. We come from the sky. We are called Fludgelings. Our home is on the planet Fludge."

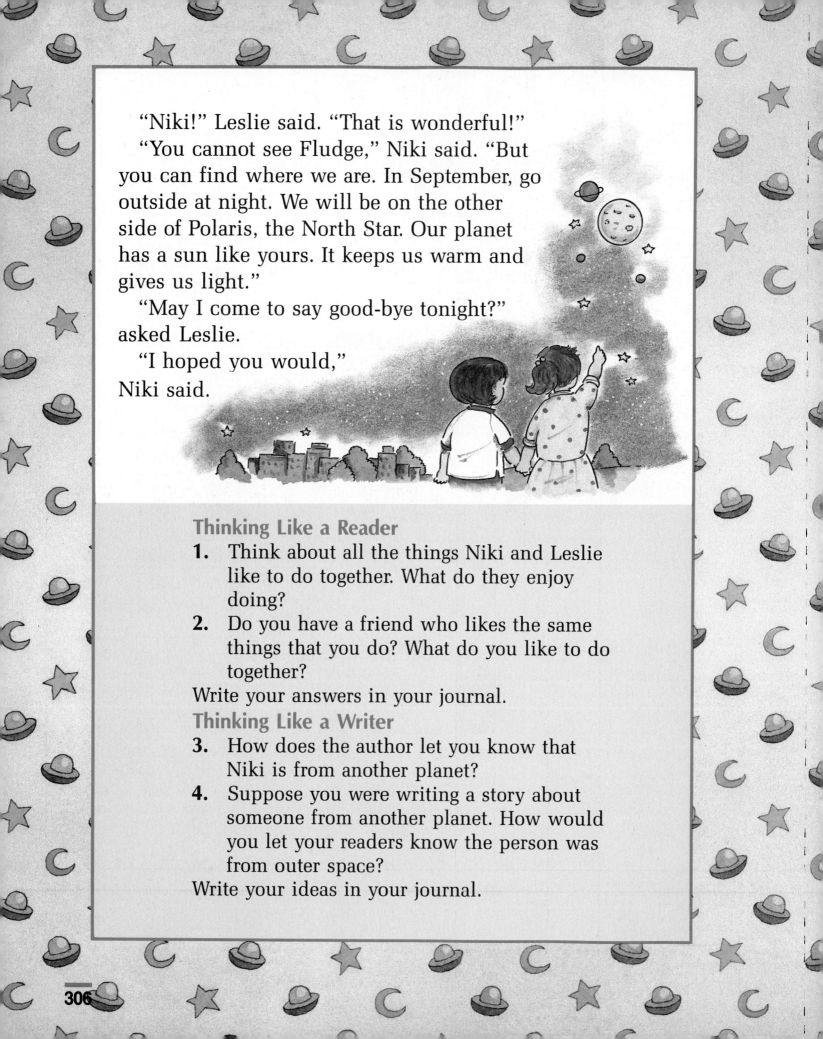

"Niki!" Leslie said. "That is wonderful!"

"You cannot see Fludge," Niki said. "But you can find where we are. In September, go outside at night. We will be on the other side of Polaris, the North Star. Our planet has a sun like yours. It keeps us warm and gives us light."

"May I come to say good-bye tonight?" asked Leslie.

"I hoped you would," Niki said.

Thinking Like a Reader

1. Think about all the things Niki and Leslie like to do together. What do they enjoy doing?

2. Do you have a friend who likes the same things that you do? What do you like to do together?

Write your answers in your journal.

Thinking Like a Writer

3. How does the author let you know that Niki is from another planet?

4. Suppose you were writing a story about someone from another planet. How would you let your readers know the person was from outer space?

Write your ideas in your journal.

Brainstorm *Vocabulary*

Make a class list of words about outer space. Write any new words in a personal word list.

Talk It Over *Start a Book Club in Class*

A book club is a good way to talk about books. Start a class book club. Draw a picture that shows what happens in a book you like. Share your picture with classmates. Talk about your book and tell why you like it.

Quick Write *You Are the Author*

Imagine that you are writing a new book about Leslie and Niki. In your journal, write several sentences that tell about your book.

Idea Corner *Think About Books*

What book would you like to share with others? In your journal, make a list of books you like.

PICTURES  *SEEING LIKE A WRITER*

Finding Ideas for Writing
Look at the pictures. Think about what you see.
What ideas for writing a book report do the pictures give you?
Write your ideas in your journal.

PICTURES: Ideas for Writing a Book Report

1 GROUP WRITING: A Book Report

When you write a book report, your **purpose** is to share a book you have read. What will your audience want to know?

- Title and Author
- About the Book (Summary)
- Your Opinion

Title and Author

A book report must tell the title and the author. Read this book report. Find the title and author.

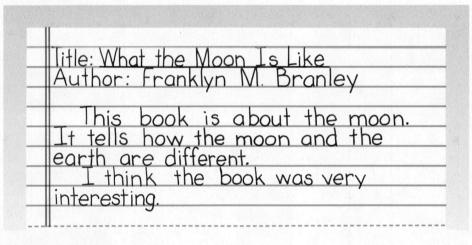

Title: What the Moon Is Like
Author: Franklyn M. Branley

   This book is about the moon. It tells how the moon and the earth are different.
   I think the book was very interesting.

Guided Practice:

Finding the Title and the Author

As a class, write the titles and authors of some books you have read.

About the Book/Your Opinion

The sample book report tells what the book is about and what the writer thinks about the book. What the writer thinks is called an **opinion**. When you write a book report, tell what the book is about. Then give your opinion of the book.

Putting a Book Report Together

Now, think about how you would put the parts of a book report together.

Here is how Dana began her book report.

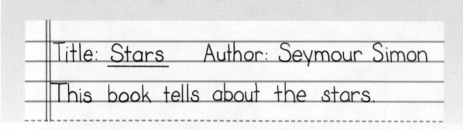

Title: <u>Stars</u>   Author: Seymour Simon

This book tells about the stars.

What does Dana need to add?

Guided Practice: Writing a Book Report

Think about a book that you have read. Write a book report. Include all the parts.

Checklist: A Book Report

Complete this checklist.

CHECKLIST

✔ Purpose and audience

✔ Title   ✔ _____

✔ Author   ✔ _____

2 THINKING AND WRITING: Telling Fact from Opinion

You know the parts of a book report. In one part of a book report, you tell about the book. You use **facts** about the book. In another part of a book report, you tell your **opinion**. You tell what you think of the book.

Wayne planned to write a report. He wrote these notes.

> 1. This book tells about Jupiter.
> 2. I think it is the best book about space ever.
> 3. I liked the photographs.
> 4. Jupiter is the largest planet.

Thinking Like a Writer

- Which sentences tell about the book?
- Which sentences tell what Wayne thinks about the book?

The first and fourth sentences are facts. They can be checked. The second and third sentences are opinions. They tell what Wayne thought about the book.

When you write a book report, be sure to tell about the book. Tell your opinion of the book, too.

THINKING APPLICATION Telling Fact from Opinion

Pam wants to write a book report about The Moon by Michael Jay. Help Pam with her report. Label each of her sentences either **fact** or **opinion**.

1. This book is all about the moon.

- -

2. I think Michael Jay is a great author.

- -

3. He compares the moon and the earth.

- -

4. The pictures are excellent.

- -

5. There are pictures of the moon's surface.

- -

3 INDEPENDENT WRITING: A Book Report

Prewrite: Step 1

You know that a book report should tell about the book. It should tell what you think about the book, too.

Kira wanted to write about a book her classmates might want to read.

Choosing a Topic

First, Kira made a list of some good books.
Next, she thought about each book.
Last, she decided which book her classmates might like.

Comets
by Martyn Hamer

The Planets in Our Solar System
by Franklyn M. Branley

Comets, Asteroids, and Meteors
by Dennis B. Fradin

Kira decided to write a book report about the second book on her list. She explored the book by making a planning chart.

Exploring Ideas: Charting Strategy

Kira looked at her chart. Then she made some changes on it.

> **Planning Chart for a Book Report**
>
> The title of the book is
>   The Planets in Our Solar System
>
> The author of the book is
>   Franklyn M. Branley
>
> Some things that happen are
>   It tells about the planets.
>   It tells about the moon.
>   It tells about comets.
>
> I like it because
>   The drawings are great.
>   It is clearly written.

Thinking Like a Writer

- What changes did Kira make? Why?

YOUR TURN JOURNAL

Follow these steps to write a book report.

- Make a list of books you have read.
- Choose the one you want to write about.
- Make a planning chart.
- Change your chart if necessary.
- Think about your purpose and audience.

Write a First Draft: Step 2

Kira made a checklist so that she could write a first draft of her report.

Here is Kira's first draft.

> Title: The Planets in Our Solar System
>
> This book is about the Planets? It tells about the moon. The author talks about comets. The author describes meteors.
>
> The Drawings are color. I like to draw. I think the author writes clear.

YOUR TURN

Write a first draft of your book report. Ask yourself these questions.

- What will my audience want to know?
- Which facts and opinions should I include?

⏱ **TIME-OUT** You might want to take some time out before you revise. Think about what you want to change.

Planning Checklist

- Remember purpose and audience.
- Title
- Author
- Summary about the book
- My opinion

Revise: Step 3

After she finished her first draft, Kira read it over to herself. Then, she shared her writing with a classmate. She wanted some ideas for making her report better.

Kira looked back at her checklist to make sure that her report was complete. She put a check next to the step she forgot. She now has a checklist to use as she revises.

Kira revised her book report. She would fix the small mistakes later.

Revising Checklist
- Remember purpose and audience.
- Title
- Author
- Summary about the book
✔ ■ My opinion

Here is Kira's revised draft.

> Title: The Planets in Our Solar System
> Author: Franklyn M. Branley
> ^nine^
> This book is about the ^ Planets? It
> tells about the moon. The author talks
> ^and^
> about comets. The ^ author describes
> meteors.
> ~~I liked this book.~~
> ^The~~ The Drawings are color. I like to
> draw. I think the author writes
> clear.

WISE
WORD
CHOICE

Thinking Like a Writer

- Which sentences did Kira revise?
- Do you think Kira's changes made her report better? Why or why not?

YOUR TURN

Read your book report. Ask yourself these questions. Then revise your book report.

- Have I included all the parts of a book report?
- How can I improve my writing?

Proofread: Step 4

Kira knew that her report would not be complete until she proofread it. She used this proofreading checklist.

Here is part of Kira's proofread report.

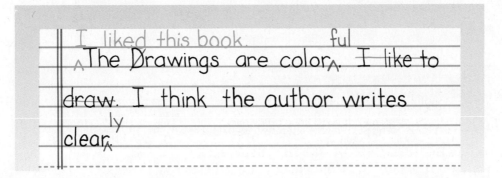

YOUR TURN

Proofreading Practice

Proofread this paragraph. Use proofreading marks to correct the mistakes. Then write the paragraph correctly on a piece of paper.

> I like the Book very much. The pictures of brave and fear astronauts are great The author writes clear, too.

Proofreading Checklist
- Did I indent each paragraph?
- Did I use capital letters correctly?
- Did I use the correct end marks?

Applying Your Proofreading Skills

Now proofread the book report you wrote. Read your checklist again. Then review **The Grammar Connection** and **The Mechanics Connection**. Use proofreading marks to correct your mistakes.

THE GRAMMAR CONNECTION

Remember these rules about adverbs.

- An **adverb** tells more about a verb.
- An **adverb** can tell <u>when</u>, <u>where</u>, or <u>how</u>.
  Now we **slowly** look around the library.

Check your report. Have you used adverbs correctly?

THE MECHANICS CONNECTION

Remember these rules about writing titles.

- Use **capital letters** to begin the first word and each important word in a title.
- Underline all the words in the title of a book.
  <u>**The Sky Is Full of Stars**</u>

Proofreading Marks

∧   Add

—   Take out

≡   Make a capital letter

/   Make a small letter

WRITING PROCESS

Publish: Step 5

Kira decided to share her book report with her classmates. She copied her book report neatly. Then she tacked it on the bulletin board. Many children asked her about the book. They wanted to read the book, too.

YOUR TURN

Make a final copy of your book report for your classmates. Here are some other ways to share your report.

SHARING SUGGESTIONS

Make a book jacket for your book report. Fold a large piece of paper in half. Draw a picture on the outside. Paste your report inside.	Write your book report for a class newspaper.	Make a puppet of someone in your book. Use the puppet while reading your book report to your class.

4 SPEAKING AND LISTENING: Giving an Oral Report

You can use what you know about writing a book report to give a talk about a book.

First, make a note card to use for your talk. Write down the title and the author of the book. Then, tell what the book is about. Last, tell how you feel about the book.

Notes

Title: The Moon
Author: Seymour Simon

It gives facts about the moon.
It explains how astronauts work on the moon.
This is an interesting book.
I love the beautiful photographs.

Use these guidelines when you give a talk.

> **SPEAKING GUIDELINES:** Giving an Oral Report
>
> 1. Tell the title and the author of the book.
> 2. Tell what the book is about.
> 3. Tell your opinion.
> 4. Look at your listeners.
> 5. Speak in a loud, clear voice.

■ Why is it important to include the title and the author when I tell about a book?

■ How will my opinion help my listeners?

SPEAKING APPLICATION Giving an Oral Report

Choose a book that you have read. Make a note card to use when you give your talk about the book. Use the speaking guidelines to help you prepare.

Use these guidelines when you listen to your classmates give their book reports.

LISTENING GUIDELINES: Giving an Oral Report

1. Listen for the title of the book.
2. Listen for the author of the book.
3. Listen for some facts about the book.
4. Listen for the opinion of the speaker.

5 WRITER'S RESOURCES: The Parts of a Book

A book has parts. A page in the front of a book gives the title and the author.

You also find a **table of contents** in the front of a book. A table of contents lists what is in the book. It tells on what page each part, or chapter, begins.

Chapter number   Name of chapter

1.	The Nine Planets	1
2.	The Sun	25
3.	The Moon	32

Page on which chapter begins

 Use the table to answer each question.

1. What is the title of Chapter 2?

- -

2. On which page does Chapter 3 begin?

- -

WRITING APPLICATION Parts of a Book

Turn to the **table of contents** in this book. Write the first page number and the name of the first lesson on adverbs.

WRITER'S RESOURCES:
Using the Library

    The **library** is the best place to find books. You use a **library card** to borrow books.

    A library has both **fiction** and **nonfiction** books. Fiction books tell about people and things that are made up. Nonfiction books tell facts.

    A library also has magazines and newspapers. Some libraries have records, tapes, films, and computers.

 Write the answer to each question.

1. What things besides books can you find at the library?

- -

2. What must you have to borrow books?

- -

3. What kind of a book tells facts about the moon?

- -

4. What kind of a book tells about purple space creatures?

- -

WRITING APPLICATION The Library

Go to your school or local library. Find and write the title and the author of both a fiction book and a nonfiction book about outer space.

Writing About Mathematics

Astronauts need to know about mathematics. When you think of mathematics, you think of numbers. Numbers can show us amounts, or how many.

ACTIVITIES

Picture Numbers Look at the chart made by some students. It tells how many children liked nonfiction and fiction books about space. Talk about the chart with your class. What does it tell you?

Type of book about space	Number who liked it
Fiction	15
Nonfiction	12

Write About Numbers Work with your class to complete the chart below. First, list things about space. Then, have the class vote for each item. Add up the votes for each item. Last, write the totals in the chart.

Our favorite things in space	Number who like it

Respond to Literature Astronauts use numbers. Read this paragraph from *Zero Is Not Nothing* by Mindel and Harry Sitomer. Then imagine that you are an astronaut who has just taken off in a rocket. Write a letter to a friend about your experience.

Zero Is Not Nothing

When a rocket is being sent into space, the countdown ends . . . 5 4 3 2 1 Blast Off. As the flight begins, the count is continued 1 2 3 4 5. . . .

Blast Off is the zero point separating the time *before* the rocket takes off from the time *after* the rocket takes off.

UNIT CHECKUP

LESSON **Group Writing: A Book Report** (page 310)
On a separate sheet of paper, list the parts of
this report that are missing.

Title: <u>Journey into a Black Hole</u>
I think this book was great.

LESSON **Thinking: Telling Fact from Opinion** (page 312)
Circle the sentence that is a fact.
- The book has exciting pictures.
- The book tells how big Mars is.

LESSON **Writing a Book Report** (page 314)   Imagine
that you write book reports for a local newspaper.
Write a book report on your favorite book.

LESSON **Speaking and Listening** (page 322)   On a
separate sheet of paper, write four things that
you should include in an oral book report.

LESSON **Parts of a Book/Using the Library** (page 324)
Circle the word that correctly completes
each sentence.

1.   A (fiction, nonfiction) book tells facts.

2.   The table of contents is at the (front, back)
of a book.

You have learned that books and book reports can help us to learn things. Look at the picture below. Talk about what is happening with your classmates. What are the astronauts giving the robot?

Which things about your life on earth would you want to tell a space robot?

- Brainstorm for some ideas with your classmates.
- Draw a picture about life on earth and write a sentence to go with it.
- Gather all the pictures together and make a class book.
- Write the title <u>Life on Earth</u> on the cover of the book.

WRITER'S REFERENCE
C O N T E N T S

HANDBOOK

Sentences

A **sentence** is a group of words that tells a complete thought.

The fruit is fresh.
Where did you buy it?

Every sentence begins with a capital letter.

Stories are fun to write.
Did you read my story?

There are four kinds of sentences.

A **statement** is a sentence that tells something.
A statement ends with a **period**.

Three ducks sat in the grass**.**
My friend fed them**.**

A **question** is a sentence that asks something.
A question ends with a **question mark**.

Why are you awake**?**
Did you sleep well**?**

A **command** is a sentence that tells or asks someone to do something.
A command ends with a **period**.

   Please come in.
   Shut the door.

An **exclamation** is a sentence that shows strong feeling.
An exclamation ends with an **exclamation mark**.

   What a lovely garden!
   Wow, that is a big tree!

The words in a sentence must be in an order that makes sense.

   This order does not make sense:

     lovely a That song. was

   This order makes sense:

     That was a lovely song.

Every sentence has two parts.

   <u>Jay and Ilana</u>   <u>write poems.</u>
      subject   predicate
   <u>My teacher</u> <u>reads many books.</u>

Nouns

A **noun** names a person, place, or thing.

The boy saw the shell at the beach .

person   thing   place

Special nouns for people, pets, and places begin with capital letters.

Tina Dow	Flappy	Elm Road
Uncle Dave	Bay City	Hill Park

Nouns that name days, months, and holidays begin with capital letters.

Friday   April   Flag Day

A noun can name more than one. Most nouns add **s** to name more than one.

trucks   birds   girls

Nouns that end with **s**, **ss**, **ch**, **sh**, and **x** add **es** to name more than one.

buses   dresses   ranches

dishes   boxes

Some nouns change their spelling to name more than one.

one **foot**	one **man**	one **child**
four **feet**	six **men**	ten **children**

Verbs

A **verb** is a word that shows action.

My sister **jogs** every day.

Add **s** to most verbs to tell what one person or thing does now.

One	he laughs
Tom **laughs** at the story.	
More than one	they laugh
Mary, Bill, and I **laugh**.	

Add **ed** to most verbs to tell about actions in the past.

Now	Past
laugh	laughed
crash	crashed
lift	lifted
talk	talked
paint	painted

Some verbs have special forms.

Verb	Now	Past
be	am, is, are	was, were
do	do, does	did
see	see, sees	saw
come	come, comes	came
go	go, goes	went
run	run, runs	ran
give	give, gives	gave
sing	sing, sings	sang

The verb **have** also has special forms.

I or you	have
I **have** two birds.	
One person or thing	has
Miri **has** three cats.	
More than one person or thing	have
The cats **have** brown ears.	

Adjectives

An **adjective** is a word that describes a noun.

> I like that **fluffy** pillow.
> The **big** bed is soft.

Some adjectives tell <u>how</u> <u>many</u>.

> Ted lost **six** pennies.
> **Several** cars passed us.

The words **a** and **an** are special adjectives. Use **a** before a word that begins with a consonant sound.

> **a** store

Use **an** before a word that begins with a vowel sound.

> **an** apple

Add **er** to an adjective to compare two nouns.

> Don is short**er** than Tony.

Add **est** to an adjective to compare more than two nouns.

> Ben is the short**est** boy of all.

Pronouns

A **pronoun** is a word that takes the place of a noun or nouns.

she	**he**	**they**	**it**	**we**
Jan	Ed	Jan and Ed	ring	Ed and I

Use the pronoun **I** in the subject part of a sentence. Write **I** with a capital letter.

I went to the beach.

Use the pronoun **me** after an action verb.

Aunt Ruth gave **me** the vase.

Use the pronoun **we** in the subject part of a sentence.

We are late today.

Use the pronoun **us** after an action verb.

Grandma took **us** home.

Adverbs

An **adverb** tells more about a verb.

Some adverbs tell <u>when</u>.

Yesterday we saw a play.

Some adverbs tell <u>where</u>.

The bird was **nearby**.

Some adverbs tell <u>how</u>.

The kitten ran **quickly**.

DICTIONARY

A a

afraid A feeling of fear or fright.
   synonym: scared

alphabet The letters we use to make words.

answer The words you say or write in
   reply to a question.
      synonym: reply
      antonym: question

B b

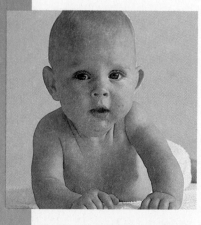

baby A very young child.

barn A farm building for horses and cows.

barnyard The land near or around a barn.

beach The land at the edge of the ocean or
   other body of water.
      synonym: shore

beautiful Very pretty to see or hear.
      synonyms: pretty, lovely
      antonym: ugly

beginning The first part of something.
      synonyms: start, opening
      antonyms: end, finish

birthday The day a person was born.

bluebird A small songbird with blue
   feathers.

boy A child who will grow up to be a man.
antonym: girl

butterfly An insect with a thin body and brightly colored wings.

C c

careless Without care. Not thinking about what you say or do.
synonym: thoughtless
antonyms: careful, thoughtful

city A place where many people live and work. It usually has tall buildings.

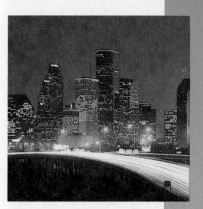

clue A key to help you find an answer to a problem or a mystery.
synonym: hint

come To move toward someone or something.
antonym: go

country The land outside cities and towns.

crow A large bird with black feathers.

D d

dark With little or no light.

dictionary A book that tells the meaning of words. The words are listed in ABC order.

different Not alike or the same.
antonym: alike, same

doghouse   A little house for a dog.

draw   To make a picture using pencils, crayons, markers, or pens.

E e

ending   The last part of something.
   synonym: finish
   antonym: beginning

event   Something that happens.

F f

father   A male parent.
   antonym: mother

field   A flat piece of land. It can be used for growing things.

first   Coming before everything or everyone.
   antonym: last

four   The number after three and before five.

-ful   A suffix that means "full of."

funny   Something that causes laughter.
   synonyms: silly, joyful
   antonyms: sad, joyless

G g

garden   A place where flowers or vegetables grow.

giant   A make-believe creature that is very huge and strong.

girl   A child who will grow up to be a woman.
   antonym: boy

goldfish   A small fish that has an orange or gold color. A goldfish can be kept as a pet.

H h

haystack   A pile of hay.

helpful   Giving help.
   synonym: useful

holiday   A special day when most people do not work and children do not go to school.

I i

information   Facts about something.

invitation   A written or spoken request to come somewhere or do something.

island   A body of land that has water all around it.

J j

jet   An airplane that uses a stream of hot gas to move.

job   Work, or something that has to be done.

joyful Filled with joy.
   synonyms: happy, funny
   antonyms: sad, joyless

jungle Land in a hot, damp place that is covered with trees, vines, and other growing things.

K k

kind Ready to help and do good deeds.
   synonyms: nice, gentle
   antonym: mean

kite A toy that flies on the end of a string.

knock To hit or tap something.

know To clearly understand or be sure about something.

L l

last Coming after everything or everyone.
   antonym: first

left The side that is opposite the right side.
   antonym: right

-less A suffix that means "without."

letter 1. One of the twenty-six parts of the alphabet. 2. A message that is written.

library   A room or building with books, magazines, and newspapers. A library might also have records, tapes, and films.

listen   To pay attention in order to hear something.

M m

middle   The part that comes between the beginning and the ending.
  synonym: center

month   One of the twelve parts of a year.

mother   A female parent.

N n

neighbor   Someone who lives next door or nearby.

next   Coming right after another.

number   A word that tells how many.

O o

ocean   The body of salt water that covers much of the earth.
  synonym: sea

once   At one time.

one   The number after zero and before two.

order   The way in which a group of things is written or told.

P p

paint 1. A liquid used to color something. 2. To cover something or make a picture with paint.

picture A painting, drawing, or photograph.

place 1. A location. 2. To put in a location.

play 1. A story that is acted out. 2. To do something for fun.

Q q

quarter A coin that is worth twenty-five cents.

quick Fast; not slow.

R r

rainbow A curved line of colors in the sky. It is seen when sunlight passes through raindrops.

re- A prefix that means "again," or "back."

refill To fill again.

reread To read again.

ride To sit on something as it moves.

right 1. The side that is opposite the left side. 2. Correct, not wrong.
  antonyms: 1. left
                    2. wrong

road   A long strip of ground or pavement used for travel.
    synonym: street

rocket   A spacecraft that is shot through the air by the burning of hot gases.

round   Shaped like a ball or circle.

S s

sad   Not happy.
    synonym: unhappy
    antonyms: happy, glad

scary   Something that causes fear or fright.
    synonym: frightening

school   A place for teaching and learning.

season   One of four parts of the year, each lasting three months: spring, summer, fall, and winter.

square   A shape with four sides that are the same length.

store   A place for buying and selling things.
    synonym: shop

sunlight   The light from the sun.

T t

tiny   Very small in size.
    synonym: small
    antonyms: huge, large

to   In the direction of.
antonym: from

too   Also; as well as.

travel   To go from one place to another place.

two   The number after one and before three.

U u

un-   A prefix that means "not," or "opposite of."

unable   The opposite of able; not able.

unhappy   The opposite of happy; sad.
antonyms: happy, glad

unlock   The opposite of lock; to open.

V v

valley   The low land between hills or mountains.

van   A covered truck used for moving things.

village   A group of houses. It is usually smaller than a town.

visit   To travel to see a person or a place.

W w

walk   To move by placing one foot in front of the other.

warm   Having some heat; not cold.
  antonym: cool

wood   The hard part of a tree that makes up the trunk and branches. It is used for building, creating fuel, and making paper.

X x

X ray   A photograph made with X rays. It shows the bones of the body.

xylophone   A musical instrument that is made up of a row or rows of wooden bars. It is played by striking the bars with a wooden hammer.

Y y

year   Twelve months in a row.

yesterday   The day before today.

Z z

zebra   An animal that looks like a horse. It has a coat of black and white stripes.

zoo   A park where people can look at animals in cages or fenced-in areas.

zoom   To move or rise quickly.

THE WRITING PROCESS

Prewriting

- Choose a purpose and audience.
- Pick a topic for your purpose and audience.
- Find ideas about your topic. You could brainstorm, make a cluster, or make a list.

Writing a First Draft

- Use your prewriting ideas to write a draft.
- Do not worry about making mistakes.

Revising

- Read your draft. Talk about it with a friend.
- Ask yourself these questions.

  What else will my audience want to know?
  Is my purpose clear?

Proofreading

- Read your revised draft.
- Ask yourself these questions.

  Did I use correct paragraph form?
  Did I use capital letters and end marks correctly?

Publishing

- Make a final, clean copy of your draft.
- Share your writing with your audience.

LETTER MODELS

You can use these models to help you when you write.

Invitation

2 Dale Lane

Tracy, California 95376   **HEADING**

May 8, 1992

Dear June,   **GREETING**

Please come to my Flag Day party on Sunday, June 14, at 1:00 P.M. We will have a   **BODY** picnic in my backyard. Everyone will get a flag to take home. I hope you can come.

Your friend,   **CLOSING**

Barry   **SIGNATURE**

Thank-You Letter

Dear Brian, **GREETING**

    Thank you for the wonderful sweater you
sent me for my birthday. The colors are so
bright and exciting. I can't wait to wear it to **BODY**
school. Maybe I will send you a picture of
me wearing it.

Your friend, **CLOSING**

Aaron **SIGNATURE**

GLOSSARY

OF WRITING, GRAMMAR, AND LITERARY TERMS

WRITING TERMS

audience   the reader or readers for whom the writer is writing

descriptive details   details in a description that tell how things look, sound, taste, feel, or smell

detail sentences   sentences in a paragraph that tell more about the main idea

first draft   the first writing of a composition. When you write a first draft, you put down your ideas on paper.

main-idea sentence   the sentence that tells the main idea of a paragraph

personal narrative   a piece of writing in which the writer tells about something that he or she did

prewriting   the stage in the writing process in which the writer decides what to write. The writer thinks about purpose and audience, picks a topic, and explores ideas about the topic.

prewriting strategies   the ways a writer explores ideas before writing the first draft

• charting   a way to gather ideas under different headings. Charts can be written in different ways to make ideas clear.

Planning Chart for a Book Report

The title of the book is
    The Planets in Our Solar System

The author of the book is
    Franklyn M. Branley

Some things that happen are
    It tells about the planets.
    It tells about the moon.

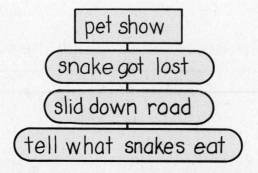

pet show

snake got lost

slid down road

tell what snakes eat

- **clustering**   a way to explore ideas by gathering details that tell about the writing topic

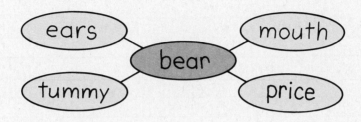

- **drawing**   a way to get ideas by drawing a picture of the writing topic

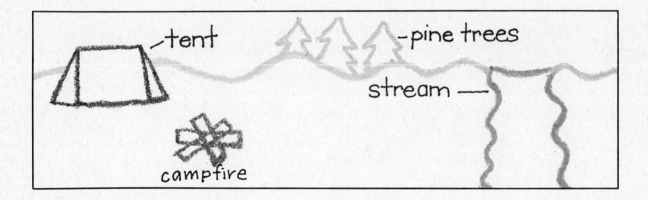

• **question chart**   a way to gather ideas by answering the five "W" questions

Who   a girl
Where   a big city
When   Thanksgiving Day
What   The girl goes to a parade.
        She grabs a balloon and
        flies away.
How   She lands when the wind stops.

proofread   to correct mistakes in punctuation, capitalization, and grammar in a writing draft

Proofreading Checklist
- Did I indent each paragraph?
- Did I use capital letters correctly?
- Did I use the correct end marks?

Proofreading Marks
∧ Add
— Take out
≡ Make a capital letter
/ Make a small letter

publish   to share a composition with an audience

purpose   the writer's reason for writing a composition

revise   to make a first draft better by adding or taking out information. A good writer thinks about purpose and audience as he or she revises.

time-order words   words that tell the order in which things happen. *First, next, then,* and *last* are some time-order words.

writing process   the steps for writing a composition. The steps are prewriting, writing a first draft, revising, proofreading, and publishing.

GRAMMAR TERMS

adjective   a word that describes a noun
                    Benny has a *new* bike.

adverb   a word that tells more about a verb
                    The clown laughed *loudly*.

command   a sentence that tells or asks someone to
                    do something
                    Clean your room.

contraction   a short form of two words
                    are not—*aren't*

exclamation   a sentence that shows strong feeling
                    What a great book this is!

noun   a word that names a person, place, or
                    thing
                    Where is your *coat*?

predicate   the part of a sentence that tells what the
                    subject does or did
                    Lucy *swam across the lake*.

pronoun   a word that takes the place of a noun
                    They take the bus to school.

question   a sentence that asks something

What time is it?

sentence   a group of words that tells a complete thought

The dog wags its tail.

statement   a sentence that tells something

I like to dance.

subject   the part of a sentence that tells who or what does something

Tad and Marta made a kite.

verb   a word that shows action

Patty *runs* across the field.

LITERARY TERMS

author   a person who writes books, plays, or articles

beginning   the first part of a story. It tells what the story is about.

end   the last part of a story. It tells how the story turns out.

fiction   writing that tells about people and things that are not real

middle   the part of a story that tells what happens between the beginning and the end

nonfiction   writing that tells about real people and things

rhyme   writing with words that sound alike
   When the sun shines round
     and *bright*,
   The snowmen melt away
     from *sight*.

INDEX